Western Approaches to Eastern Europe

To my friend Laszlo —
With cordial wishes

[signature]

New York City

4 June 1994

Western Approaches to Eastern Europe

J.F. Brown
Robert D. Hormats
William H. Luers

Edited by Ivo John Lederer

COUNCIL ON FOREIGN RELATIONS PRESS

NEW YORK

CRITICAL ISSUES

Critical Issues papers, produced under the Studies Program of the Council on Foreign Relations, are designed to provide insight on various aspects of the current foreign policy agenda of the United States as well as special perspective on certain longer term issues. The authors are generally senior fellows or others associated with the Studies Program. The intent of *Critical Issues* is to provide Council members and other readers with important papers that are informal, provocative, and easy to read.

The Council on Foreign Relations, Inc., is a nonprofit and nonpartisan organization devoted to promoting improved understanding of international affairs through the free exchange of ideas. The Council does not take any position on questions of foreign policy and has no affiliation with, and receives no funding from, the United States government. All statements of fact and expressions of opinion contained in any Council publication are the sole responsibility of the author.

This volume constitutes issues 6, 7, and 8 of the 1992 Critical Issues series.

Copyright © 1992 by the Council on Foreign Relations, Inc.
All rights reserved.
Printed in the United States of America.
ISBN 0-87609-130-3
ISSN 1040-4767

For further information please contact:

The Publications Office
Council on Foreign Relations
58 East 68th Street, New York, NY 10021

Library of Congress Cataloging-in-Publication Data

Lederer, Ivo John, 1929–
    Western approaches to Eastern Europe / J.F. Brown. Robert D. Hormats. William H. Luers : edited by Ivo John Lederer.
        p.   cm.
    Includes bibliographical references.
    ISBN 0-87609-130-3 : $14.95
    1. Europe, Eastern–Foreign relations—1989– 2. United States—Foreign relations–Europe, Eastern. 3. Europe. Eastern–Foreign relations–United States. I. Brown J.F. (James F.) II. Hormats, Robert D. III. Luers, William H. IV. Title.
    DJK51.B76   1992
    327.73047—dc20   92-16998
                                                              CIP

Cover design: Jon McEwan

CONTENTS

FOREWORD

Eastern Europe is at a critical stage as it attempts to develop workable market-driven economies and democratic societies. Some countries are further along the road than others, but the entire region is struggling to overcome the legacies of communist mismanagement and misrule. A happy outcome is by no means assured.

There is universal agreement that local resources and effort will not be enough; Western Europe and the United States must help, and in fact substantially increase the level of assistance they have provided thus far. The involvement of Western Europe is quite natural for reasons of geographic proximity and close involvement with the region over the centuries. Western Europe has much to lose if Eastern Europe disintegrates into chaos. It also has much to gain—initially an array of recoverable industries and natural resources, as well as a large and inexpensive labor pool that could serve Western economic needs and interests.

The picture is not so clear-cut for the United States: it is not immediately threatened by instability in Eastern Europe. Even so, Americans cannot be indifferent to the fate of the region, for whose freedom and prosperity this country waged the Cold War—at least in part—for over forty years. What are American interests in this troubled zone? What should American policy be there? What specific roles should the United States play in order to secure stability in Eastern Europe, and thereby throughout Europe as a whole?

To consider these and related questions, the Council on Foreign Relations held a symposium on "The United States and Eastern Europe" in New York City on 10–11 September 1991. The thirty-nine participants (See Appendix) included academic and private-sector specialists, generalists, and six distinguished guests from Eastern Europe. The discussions were probing and lively, centering on five sequential themes: "The East European Setting: The Legacies and Trends"; "The View from Eastern Europe"; "The Impact of Soviet Developments on Eastern Europe"; "U.S. Economic-Commercial and Political Interests in Eastern Europe"; and "U.S. Objectives and Policy Roles: The Economic-Political-Security Dimensions."

The three essays included in this volume—"The East European Agenda" by J.F. Brown, "An Economic Policy for the United States and the West" by Robert D. Hormats, and "Harmonizing U.S. and Western Interests" by William H. Luers—are revised versions of papers originally written for the symposium. The introduction by Ivo Lederer, who organized and directed this ambitious event, places these issues in a broader context. Together, the four pieces encapsulate the range of questions and concerns that policymakers as well as the general public must take into account in the development of a sound U.S. policy toward Eastern Europe.

Nicholas X. Rizopoulos
Vice President, Studies

ACKNOWLEDGMENTS

I am grateful to J.F. Brown, Robert D. Hormats, and William H. Luers for the time and effort they invested in the final versions of their essays. I am also grateful for the support and assistance provided by Peter Tarnoff, President of the Council on Foreign Relations, John Temple Swing, Executive Vice President, Nicholas X. Rizopoulos, Director of Studies, David Haproff, Managing Editor, Theresa Weber of the Council's Studies staff for her administrative assistance, and to both her and Audrey McInerney, also of the Studies staff, for serving so ably as rapporteurs at the symposium. A special word of heartfelt thanks to Cyrus R. Vance for taking the time to chair the symposium and for guiding its discussions with patience and wisdom.

Ivo John Lederer

INTRODUCTION: THE CONTEXT

Ivo John Lederer

The collapse of communism in Eastern Europe* and the Soviet Union is the most significant geopolitical event of our times. A nineteenth-century idea, implemented in Russia in 1917, communism in many ways became the defining force of the twentieth century. The Cold War it generated after 1945 produced a fierce struggle between two antipodal systems of values and governance, one devoted to political and economic freedom, the other to total state control. Perceived for decades as something bigger than life, communism went down and out after 1989 in a series of whimpers, not the Armageddon everyone had so long feared. It was a Potemkin system after all—a grandiose façade.

The passing of communism produced understandable euphoria, but it also produced unforeseen consequences. No one quite anticipated the difficulties inherent in the sudden rush to democracy and capitalism, whose development in the West took generations of painstaking and cumulative effort. Nor was the West

---

* "Eastern Europe" is an imperfect and contested term. Some prefer East-Central Europe, others Central and Eastern Europe, depending on whether Russia, Ukraine, and other Eastern states are considered part of Europe. A number of Polish, Czech, and other intellectuals, moreover, have long sought refuge in such terminological vanities to denote that they belong to the West and to disassociate their cultures from the East (for example the Poles and Czechs from their eastern neighbors, the Hungarians from the Romanians, the Croats from the Serbs, and so on). "Eastern Europe" is used here for the sake of convenience and is meant to include Poland, the Czech and Slovak Republic, Hungary, Romania, Bulgaria, Albania, and all the territory of former Yugoslavia. The region as a whole comprises an area of 450,000 square miles and a (1990) population of 123 million inhabitants.

prepared for the dominant European role of the newly reunified Germany, the total disintegration of the Soviet Union, or the savage civil war in Yugoslavia. Only a handful of experts understood the potential virulence of the ingrained passion of nationalism. We forgot that, as Sir Isaiah Berlin recently reminded us, "In our modern age, nationalism is not resurgent; it never died. Neither did racism. They are the most powerful movements in the world today."[1] Nationalism destroyed Yugoslavia and to a large extent the Soviet Union; it threatens the survival of the Czech and Slovak Republic. It afflicts the United Kingdom, Spain, Belgium, Canada, India, and other corners of the world; it may be a hidden element in the discord between the United States and Japan.

As a result of the events of 1989 the Europe we have known has been forever changed. The old assumptions no longer apply. The European Community (EC) is no longer the (relatively) comfortable Club of Twelve, planning to expand to a limit of, say, sixteen. The foyers of Brussels are filled with anxious candidates from the East, some of whom—Hungary, the Czech and Slovak Republic, Poland, perhaps even Slovenia and Croatia—may be, or may have to be, admitted before this decade is out. Will such East European participation turn out to be an albatross, or will it eventually add a bounty of human and material resources to the EC, turning Europe into a more formidable competitor in world markets and a more powerful voice in world affairs? Will the North-South, or rich-poor, frictions within the EC, as it exists today, be extended over the continent as a whole, with dramatically different socio-economic neighborhoods, creating a Europe A and a Europe B, even a limbo category C? No one knows the answers to these questions at this time.

Another fundamental question pertains to the role of the United States, global proconsul of the forces of democracy throughout this century. Now that "the job" appears to be done, Americans, constrained by domestic needs and psychological ennui, would like nothing better than to pull back to a "necessary minimum," but no one is quite sure what level of involvement remains necessary or what constitutes the minimum. The gut feeling that dealing with the dire straits and messiness of the East should be left to Western Europeans is offset by several elemental considerations. Most immediate and urgent is the need to bring order to the enormous nuclear arsenal of the former Soviet Union and to the process of its dismantlement. No less serious is the challenge of inducing the successor republics, including those across the vast Moslem belt, to become cooperative members of the international community. Perhaps no situation today is fraught with greater dangers—for the United States, the East European neighbors of the former Soviet Union, for Asia, indeed the world.

In Western Europe the world is witnessing a concentration of economic and political power in the hands of a reunified Germany, causing uncertainties—both East and West—as to how this power will ultimately be applied. The emotion-laden debate concerning past and present German purposes will not end soon, despite the general acceptance of Germany's "Europeanness" today. Many Europeans (in both the East and the West) fear a growing German monopoly in the East, even if it is caused by the accidents of location, size, work-efficiency, and the unwillingness (or inability) of other Western countries to step in with significant investments and expenditures. It is a progressive disequilibrium which the United States cannot ignore.

That brings us directly to the third problem the United States now confronts—namely the region that lies between Germany and the former Soviet Union. An important aspect of the situation is how the East European states relate to their neighbors to the West and East. In formulating its policy toward Eastern Europe, the United States must strike a balance between the growing power of Germany and a currently weakened Russia that will surely rise again. At the same time, we need to see Eastern Europe in a broader world context as well, for many of its problems are not unique; if the transition to democracy and free markets works there, the lessons may well be applicable elsewhere.

We have come a long way in our responses to the events of 1989. Within a year and a half of the initial celebration, Americans and

West Europeans have grown distinctly irritated by the spectacle of tribalism and talk of secession, the cacophony of historical claims and counterclaims, economic ignorance, the slow pace of reforms, and, above all, by Eastern European expectations of Western aid in the midst of growing recession everywhere. Westerners mistakenly thought that political and economic democratization in Eastern Europe would be a straight and sure line, overlooking the pervasive obsolescence created by the communist regimes, and the involuntary managerial amateurism of the post-communist leaderships. More recently, irritation has given way to a weary but also more serious appreciation of the problems the East Europeans face. The East Europeans, on the other hand, have come to understand that the United States and Western Europe have pressing agendas of their own, cannot afford a massive new Marshall Plan, and, above all, that the Western private sector is unlikely to invest heavily in a region with so many political problems and uncertainties.

No single development in Eastern Europe helped crystallize Western perceptions more than the ongoing crisis in Yugoslavia. Because in many ways it is a microcosm of the region as a whole, the Yugoslav case deserves special attention. The human tragedy that has taken place and the political intricacies that will take years to sort out provide a cautionary tale for what could easily happen elsewhere, if reason and wise statesmanship are not applied in time. The Yugoslav problem is not one of recent vintage, of 1989, 1945, or even of 1918. That is because the border between Serbs and Croats is not merely the border between two ethnic groups or nationalities. It is also the border between Roman Catholicism and Eastern Orthodoxy, which have been locked in animosity for an entire millennium; it is the old border between Hapsburg Europe and the Ottoman Empire; it is the border between industrial development and an agrarian way of life. Psychologically it is the obdurate Great Divide, a symbol of the broader disjunction between the western and eastern segments of Eastern Europe as a whole.

In the case of Yugoslavia, another, more specific, bone of contention has long been at work as well. When, during the First World

War, the Serbs, Croats, and Slovenes came together for the first time to construct a common statehood—which, with the help of Allied victory, they proclaimed on December 1, 1918—they immediately clashed over the future of their relationship. The Serbs demanded, and soon enforced, a centralized national framework, while the Croats and Slovenes sought a federative partnership. That key difference has plagued their relationship ever since: in the 1920s and 1930s; exploding into an atavistic civil war in 1941–45; resurfacing as an issue under Tito in the late 1960s; and as a new and lethal paroxysm in 1991. To complicate matters further, the present Yugoslav crisis was set off by Serbian repression of the Moslem Albanians in Kosovo. It is not likely to end without a solution to the Kosovo issue. The larger Moslem factor is now on the agenda too and cannot be ignored.

Whether the reciprocal excesses among the Yugoslavs during World War II—especially the mass killing of Serbs by Croat fascists—and the quantitatively different atrocities precipitated by Serbia's attack on Croatia in 1991 could have been averted by a more sensible management of the Yugoslav state from 1918 on may be a moot question today, but the Yugoslav case is worth taking into account, on two grounds. First, it illustrates the depth and stubbornness of certain historic hatreds, resentments, and distrusts, which are also visible among former Soviet nationalities, and between Slovaks and Czechs, Hungarians and Romanians, and Greeks and Turks. This does not mean that violence will inevitably break out all over Eastern Europe, but in certain cases that possibility lurks just beneath the surface. Second, it helps explain why the EC has faltered in dealing with a situation so fraught with danger for the continent as a whole.

West Europeans have only recently managed to bury (more or less) their own historical hatchets and learn to resolve peaceably their own local and cross-border disputes. Without economic prosperity and the helpful hand of the United States, ancient antipathies might still, or once more, run rampant on the West European scene. The EC has proved inadequate in dealing with the Yugoslav

challenge because at critical junctures West European governments have continued to think and behave like the nation-states of
yore. Some, such as the United Kingdom and Spain, have been
reluctant to concede the legitimacy of secession in Yugoslavia, for
fear of its impact on their own home fronts. Also, during the last
phases of Gorbachev's rule they did not wish to encourage the
breakup of the Soviet Union. More important, however, has been
the instinctive tendency to "side" with historical friends or allies.
For the French, therefore, it was perhaps natural to look more
benignly upon their old friends the Serbs, just as the Germans and
Austrians are prone to favor the Slovenes and the Croats. The
Italians, too, hope to reestablish their influence in Hungary and
southeast Europe, and at the same time contain the spread of
German influence. Such predilections do not make for an effective
and unified EC voice and policy.

Because the United Nations embodies the authority of the
world community, it stands a better chance of separating the com-
batants in Yugoslavia than does the EC, thereby paving the way to
negotiations and an eventual solution. In this process, however,
the UN, the EC, and the United States will need to work together if
progress is to be made. If the current UN experiment in the former
Yugoslavia helps bring about a settlement, a valuable precedent
may well be set for the entire East.

* * *

Although we often think of it as comprising one economic and
geostrategic area, the countries of Eastern Europe vary greatly in
terms of their size and topography, history, ethnic composition,
culture, economic resources, political habits, and linkages abroad.
At one time or another, most of these countries enjoyed longer or
briefer periods of glory, before they were destroyed or conquered by
the Russians, Germans, Austrians, or Ottoman Turks. In the tenth
century and again in the thirteenth, the Bulgarian Empire held
sway in the Balkans, as did the Serbian Empire for much of the
fourteenth century. The Croats held an extensive kingdom from
925 to 1102. At the turn of the thirteenth century Hungary ex-

tended from southern Poland to the Adriatic. In the mid-fifteenth century the Czech kingdom (Bohemia) was the epicenter of European trade and learning. At the time of the Peace of Westphalia in 1648 the Kingdom of Poland was the largest empire in Europe (save for that of the Ottoman Turks). By the late eighteenth century, however, all vestiges of independence in Eastern Europe were eradicated by the surrounding empires; until 1918 the region, in effect, became colonialized. Between the two World Wars there was a brief interlude of independence—not enough time to develop sound mechanisms for self-governance.

Small wonder, then, that Eastern Europeans seem transfixed by their more distant pasts. History is the mirror through which all peoples see and adjudge themselves. The bleaker the present, the greater the need to recall past greatness.[2] It is not a vanity peculiar to the nations of Eastern Europe. Italians of only yesterday held up ancient Rome as a weapon to mobilize their society; in our own day, Colonel Nasser and the Shah of Iran played upon visions of ancient Egypt and Persia as a placebo against their populations' lassitude; the unrelenting French penchant for past grandeur is a variation on the same theme. In this country, the Founding Fathers and the Constitution are invoked to shepherd us in our daily lives. Israelis and Arabs feed by the hour on the irretrievable past. History is everyone's companion, serving different purposes, producing different effects.

No less is true in the case of Russia. In Russia, however, economic and political servitude was not imposed from the outside; it evolved domestically as the system and ideology of autocracy, which in one form or another—except for the flicker of a decade after the Revolution of 1905—governed Tsarist Russian and then Soviet society. The roots of autocracy may have been defensive, born of the necessity to survive the onslaught of Mongolian and other hordes and subsequent incursions from the "civilized" West. The endless foreign invasions, internal revolutions, and civil wars produced a fixation with external and internal security and became the rationale for imperial expansionism: the appetite, perceived as need, to conquer or at least control adjacent territories to the east and west, until the Tsarist empire extended from the Pacific Ocean to the heart of Europe. One forgets that in the mid-eighteenth century Russian armies occupied Berlin, and Paris in 1814, and that some Tsarist geostrategicians entertained visions of such faraway places as Madagascar, India, and Ethiopia and of dominating the closer jewel, Constantinople. Around 1848 the Tsarist diplomat Fedor Tiutchev, in a poem called "Russian Geography," saw the frontiers of Russia as demarcated by seven great rivers: the Neva, the Volga, the Euphrates, the Ganges, the Elbe, the Danube, and the Nile.

This is not to argue that such notions were the dominant fare of Russian thought and behavior, for they were not, but they were an extremist strand throughout. Nor do these sentiments animate the Russia of today, but they reflect a past impulse of which Europeans, East and West, are ontologically conscious, and which they fear. The fact is that Russia is used to being a major factor in world affairs. That habit, interrupted from time to time by spasms of internal adversity, is now ingrained. If fledgling democracy falters, it might well be succeeded by a nationalistic and xenophobic Russia, and all the consequences that might derive from that.

Right now the Russians have little reason to look upon their recent or more remote past with a kind eye. Eastern Europeans, on the other hand, are making use of history to bolster their self-esteem, or, in certain cases, to settle ancient scores. The trouble is that a fixation with the past tends to distort present realities. There is no room in Eastern Europe today for any empire of a millennium ago. As empires in this region rose and fell, they overlapped in their control of territory. Populations shifted, in some cases intermarried, creating border zones of mixed ethnic groups and a host of problematic territorial claims and counterclaims. That, coupled with traditions that place a higher premium on the rule of force than on negotiation and compromise, represents today the most negative legacy of the past. This does not mean that East Europeans are not learning fast. They are coming to understand that becoming an integral part of Europe means adopting the rules and standards of behavior that have brought Western Europe political tranquility and economic success.

The effort to develop the institutions and habits of Western political democracy is being undertaken against the backdrop of economic crisis. We are told that the "reconstruction and integration of Russia and Eastern Europe into the Western economy" will cost at least $180 billion a year for ten years, if not more.[3] Whether this figure is correct, too modest, or overblown is being hotly debated by professional economists. Whatever the actual requirement, it will be staggering. Another important point is that in such critical circumstances, a weary and disheartened population is more vulnerable to populist exhortations, promises of easy solutions and calls for law and order.

We assumed that with the collapse of communism in 1989 all former communists would pass away from the scene. Most of them have, but certainly not all. Yesterday's valiant dissidents and anti-communists hold the helm nearly everywhere, yet elsewhere former party stalwarts are still in charge. Renamed with acceptable socialist and democratic labels, several former communist parties are present in national parliaments, garnering disturbing percentages of the popular vote. Their mischief potential should not be discounted. Behind them stands a presently inert phalanx of former party faithful, smarting at having fallen from power into disgrace, a new *lumpenbourgeoisie* that could someday rally to the cause of some dark figure on a white horse. This is not a prediction; the very idea seems farfetched. And yet. . . . Given a particular set of circumstances and enough popular despair, nothing can be excluded, not even the appearance of some latter-day Marshal Pilsudski or Admiral Horthy. In Poland today the popularity of General Jaruzelski is on the rise. Ordinary people seek economic security; democracy is not an adequate substitute for food. That is what the Wałęsas and the Havels fear today, and their mood is sober as they cope with the domestic disarray in their countries.

Yet for all of its problems and uncertainties, the East European landscape is far from bleak. Enormous strides have already been made. The "pull" of the EC is instilling discipline and hope. Everyone longs for the friendship of America, and its political and economic benefits. No one wants to revert to the dependent status of the 1930s or the *Pax Sovietica* of more recent years. The East European youth is internationalized; the managerial class wants to be modernized. These are substantial assets, preconditions for the fulfillment of the promise of 1989.

* * *

In the United States, the public debate concerning U.S. policy toward Eastern Europe revolves around three central questions:

1. Can the countries of the region become viable market economies and enduring democracies?

2. How much help, and in what form, must America and its allies provide to help achieve these ends?

3. Ultimately, does Eastern Europe *really* matter to the United States and the world, or, put crudely, "who cares?"

Two points, at any rate, are clear. The fundamental responsibility to make things work lies with the East Europeans themselves. Their efforts, however, particularly on the economic side, cannot succeed without Western guidance, technical assistance, and private sector investments. Democracy cannot take root in the face of economic blight and hopelessness, and political stability cannot be assured without the safeguards of democracy and its turbulent yet ultimately orderly processes.

The East Europeans have had little prior experience with economic and political pluralism, although the Czechs and Hungarians have had more of it than others. On the whole, however, both the leaders and the populations in the area are groping their way through the dark. They seek—and are bombarded by—Western advice, and are ill-equipped to sort out the sensible from the self-serving. Above all, they are straining, under the tyranny of real-life deadlines, to stave off economic disaster; to deliver to their peoples on the historic promises of 1989; to qualify for membership in the EC; and to fend off German domination and possible future Russian expansionism. It is quite a mission; considering that it is being undertaken as the first historical transition from a command to a free system of society, it is nothing short of a Grand Experiment.

Where does the United States fit into all of this? A very able young Hungarian said not long ago: "The United States never had and never will have an East European policy. It had a Moscow policy, a Bonn policy, and now a Brussels policy. But not an East European policy." In the main, quite right. In this century it was Germany and then the Soviet Union that drew the United States into both World Wars and the Cold War. Therefore it was Germany and then the Soviet Union that had to be neutered. Eastern Europe, long perceived as the troublesome catalyst of war in 1914 and 1939, after 1945 became the ostensible objective of victory over Moscow in the Cold War—the banner behind which the free world could rally and keep the West mentally and materially mobilized for what actually turned into a global struggle.

Today, with the center of gravity in Europe inexorably shifting to Germany and chaos pervading the former Soviet Union, it behooves Washington to keep its focus on these two mutable scenes. If mayhem breaks out in Eastern Europe, as it has in Yugoslavia, it could create a power vacuum, tempting today's Germany and tomorrow's Russia, if not others, to fill it. Russia, sooner or later, will again be pivotal in global affairs. It remains the largest country in the world, with a military capability second only to that of the United States. Just as partnership in the EC mitigates against German unilateralism, so would a peripheral string of sound, prosperous, and territorially unambitious states act on Russia. It is thus in the American self-interest to help achieve these ends.

Healthy East European states, able to stand on their own, attached to the broader Western political economy and in amicable relations with Russia and Ukraine, are the greatest guarantee for a stable Europe. Henry Kissinger puts it in even more imperative terms:

> No issue is more urgent than to relate the former Soviet satellites of Eastern Europe to Western Europe and to NATO. At least Poland, Czechoslovakia and Hungary should be permitted to join the Community rapidly. It is hardly to the credit of the West that after talking for a generation about freedom for Eastern Europe, so little is done to vindicate it. Moreover, if a no man's land is to be avoided in Eastern Europe, NATO should leave no doubt that pressures against those countries would be treated as a challenge to Western security—whatever the formal aspects of this undertaking.[4]

It is perhaps ironic that the well-being of Russia and Eastern Europe should be so closely linked today, if only in the sense that a bankrupt and chaotic Russia poses one kind of danger for Eastern Europe and a prosperous but ambitious Russia poses another. In either case, Eastern Europe must develop sound economic and political foundations to ward off any untoward effects from its mightier neighbors to the east and, for that matter, from Germany and others in the West.

* * *

What 1989 did for Eastern Europe, 1991 did for Russia—the opening of an entirely new chapter. Their effect has been no less for the United States. The collapse of communism, as the defeat of German militarism in 1945, has justified the enormous effort this country has invested throughout the twentieth century in providing Europe and the world with a chance to live in freedom and a modicum of safety.

Now, as we survey the discouraging enormity of Eastern needs, it is important to differentiate—yet not entirely separate—the challenges posed by Russia and the other former Soviet republics on the one hand and those presented by Eastern Europe on the other. Russia—a world power that is today in the throes of a historic interregnum—is a great nuclear power that must not be ignored. Eastern Europe is critically important in other ways; apart from serious moral considerations and obligations, the region should be seen as possessing the quality of a gyroscope—a stabilizing force if it functions well, a destabilizing force if it breaks down.

Throughout the region, the United States and the West must insist on at least one basic principle of collective policy—that they will not consent to *any* changes of frontiers that are gained by force and not by a prior negotiated settlement. There are too many border disputes in the East; to allow one forced change would encourage a spate of others in the years to come.

The western half of Eastern Europe—Poland, Czechoslovakia, Hungary, perhaps Slovenia, and before very long Croatia—enjoys the preconditions for developing viable market economies: experience, the will, and skills that are being daily forged. It needs a helping push and a cushion of time to make it into the EC. The eastern half of the region—Romania, Bulgaria, Serbia, and Albania—requires more. Because this chain of states is the region of greatest volatility, it should receive much more political and economic attention than it has to date. The price tag is not likely to be very high, but the return in terms of staving off social disasters and ethnic explosions would undoubtedly be great.

Much American political capital is already at work in the region, and it is absolutely free: it is the unique popularity of the United States, the belief that the pragmatic Americans know how to attack and resolve any kind of challenge. Above all, as Eastern Europeans look to their neighbors, East and West, they are comforted by the knowledge that the United States has a clean historical record; it has no territorial designs upon the region—an area that has so frequently been coveted by larger adjacent European powers. East Europeans crave association with the EC, and by extension NATO, for reasons of economic and strategic security. They see the United States as the ultimate guarantor of both. The challenge for the United States, then, is to build on this anxious good will, to continue to make its presence felt, and not to dissipate a historic opportunity before it becomes too late.

* * *

The essays that follow address three vital aspects of U.S. policy in Eastern Europe. In the first chapter J. F. Brown provides an overview of the political, social, and psychological aspects of the situation in Eastern Europe and illustrates the endemic tensions between plans for the future and the burden of the past. He takes a sober look at the course of reform since 1989 and assesses the quality of leadership in the region and the challenges it still confronts.

The second chapter, by Robert D. Hormats, outlines a broad program of economic engagement for the United States and the European Community in Eastern Europe. He deals specifically with the extent of responsibility that should be assumed by the United States and how it would relate and interact with a joint Western commitment to rebuilding the region.

Finally, William H. Luers examines the immediate and longer term stakes of Russia, Germany, and other EC countries in Eastern Europe and analyzes how U.S. policy must take these complexities into account. In a period in which the United States must increasingly attend to its domestic affairs, in which Europe is moving from its previous accessory role in the anti-Soviet coalition to a primary role as the architect of a new continental system, in which Russia and Ukraine have yet to find their real place. U.S. policy cannot simply assert its own will, even if it had a clear-cut goal for Eastern Europe.

Yet, the United States cannot abstain from involvement in the region; to do so would guarantee retrogression, if not chaos. The United States must, instead, formulate a viable policy for working with the countries of both Western and Eastern Europe to ensure the region's stability and continued progress toward democracy and prosperity.

NOTES

[1] Nathan Gardels, "Two concepts of Nationalism: An Interview with Isaiah Berlin," *The New York Review*, Nov. 21, 1991.

[2] Here is how Stefan Zweig put it in his 1916 essay, "The Tower of Babel": "Mankind's profoundest legends are concerned with its beginnings. The symbols of origin have wonderful poetic power, and as if of their own accord they make reference to every subsequent great moment of history in which

nations renew themselves and significant epochs have their beginnings."
Austrian Information, vol. 45, no. 3, 1992, p. 6.

[3] See Leonard Silk, citing David Suratgar of Morgan Grenfell & Company, *The New York Times,* January 3, 1992.

[4] Henry Kissinger, "Europe Needs America . . . " *New York Post,* March 3, 1992.

1

THE EAST EUROPEAN AGENDA

J.F. Brown

As early as the spring of 1990, barely a few months after the Czechoslovak "velvet" revolution, a Prague daily newspaper was already registering an unease that was felt throughout Eastern Europe: "The Revolution euphoria is fading fast. The public is beginning to ask—what now?" Now, at the end of 1991, the "Revolution euphoria" has disappeared completely. The exhilaration and sense of purpose of 1989 has been replaced by impatience, anxiety, even disillusion. This essay is an attempt to analyze the reasons for this dramatic change of mood, to put developments in the Eastern European states in perspective, and to describe the most significant external factors affecting their present and their future.

All of the Soviet Union's erstwhile satellites—even Romania, the slowest and least sure—have moved definitively away from communism. But the touchstone of progress has long since become not moving away from communism, but moving toward democracy. The goal of a Western-type liberal democracy had looked relatively simple as communism was being overturned, but in the following months the Eastern Europeans were to learn how difficult and apparently thankless their chosen task was to be.

Nor has the resulting frustration been confined to Eastern Europeans. Many Westerners who enthusiastically supported the revolutions of 1989 have since responded with resignation or pat generalizations about the long list of Eastern Europe's congenital shortcoming, stemming both from their communist and precommunist past. Accordingly, they have turned away from such a troubling landscape. Granted, there were momentous enough events to distract them: the disintegration and collapse of the

16

Soviet Union; the eclipse of Gorbachev; the reunification of Germany; the crisis in the Persian Gulf. These events provided some excuse for "shelving" Eastern Europe, but its fate remains one of the world's determining issues. What happens in Eastern Europe affects the whole of Europe—and the future of the Soviet Union's successor states. The issue won't go away, and it can't be avoided.

The fate of Eastern Europe will be decided by the way a large number of interrelated problems are tackled. Not all these problems need be completely solved. Some of them are not capable of solution; at best they can be managed or contained. They also vary from country to country, in both type and degree of tractability. (Generalizations about Eastern Europe were always dangerous, even under communism.) But the problems exist everywhere, forming both the legacy of communist rule and the agenda for its successors.

The postcommunist agenda is crowded and daunting. It is also long-term, more a marathon than the 100-yard dash some fervent Eastern Europeans first assumed. It is also indivisible: the parts connect and relate. Any division of them is, therefore, arbitrary and hazardous. It is best and safest to attempt it along four lines:

1. Economic and political development;

2. Overcoming the past;

3. Nationalism and regional relations;

4. International relations.

ECONOMIC AND POLITICAL DEVELOPMENT

How, then, to achieve this Western-type liberal democracy, the pursuit of which—as the West itself knows—is so thorny? Few would disagree that the first essential is to build a new, sound, economic basis on the ruins of the old. The following economic problems give some idea of the magnitude of the problem. They are not all the fault of the communist system. Most go back well before it was installed. But communism, in its attempt to overcome the problems, only exacerbated them.

• *A collapsed economic structure.* Even the reputedly strongest Eastern European economies were in terminal crisis. Václav Havel, speaking of the Czechoslovak case—certainly the least crisis-ridden—said that, instead of a house badly needing repair, they had inherited a ruin. As for the East German economy, it will weigh down the reunited Germany for years to come.

• *Ecological catastrophe.* In some parts of Eastern Europe this problem is no longer just an economic or a social hazard; it has assumed a deadly physical dimension—no longer a question of the quality of life, but of life itself.

• *Wrecked social welfare facilities.* Once socialism's propaganda flagship, the welfare system has been deteriorating in most countries since the mid-1970s. It is hopelessly inadequate now in the face of the social upheavals caused by economic transformation.

• *Emigration.* One of the ironies of the present situation is that some of Eastern Europe's best and brightest young people are leaving for the West when they are most needed for the immense task of their country's reconstruction. Their reasons may be perfectly understandable, and many promise to return, armed with new skills and experiences to place at their country's disposal. How many will actually do so is open to question. The contrast with the situation at the end of the nineteenth and the early twentieth centuries is striking. Then, the best and the brightest tended to stay home to help build their newly independent or newly created countries, and were joined by thousands of their compatriots who had been living abroad. Today, patriotism counts for little compared with then; forty years of communism didn't do much for that or for other civic virtues. A different set of preferences and psychological impulses now prevails, and new factors, such as television and modern travel, induce a restlessness that makes past norms obsolete.

To these internal problems, three external factors should be added that have had an important bearing on Eastern Europe's economic situation:

• *The inadequacy of Western aid.* Government officials in both the United States and Western Europe vigorously deny any inadequacy. But, as both the immensity of the East Europeans' problems and their inability to cope with them unaided become more obvious, it is increasingly difficult to take such official Western protestations seriously. It is ultimately a question of priorities—of where Eastern Europe fits in the national and international scheme of things. In 1990, the city of Oakland offered more money to try to tempt the Raiders to return from their lotus-eating exile in Los Angeles than the American government gave to Poland that entire year.

• *Soviet unreliability as an economic partner.* This is examined later in a more recent context. By early 1991, this had already become a problem of disastrous proportions.

• *The Gulf War.* The effects of this crisis were secondary, but nonetheless damaging. Close economic relations with Iraq were a legacy from Warsaw Pact and Comecon days—part profit, part penetration, part socialist noblesse oblige. The virtual extinction of Iraq's economy particularly affected Bulgaria and Romania, two of Eastern Europe's weakest economies.

There is general, though not universal, agreement on the remedy for these accumulated ills: move as quickly and effectively as possible from state socialism to a market economy based on classical Western principles. These are: free prices, no subsidies, open economies to foreign investments and trade, convertible currencies, privatization, closure of unprofitable plants. The move can be made by means of "shock therapy," a quick come-what-may break for capitalism, or by "gradualism," a slower process taking into account the painful social effects of the transition involved. Poland was at first the torchbearer of shock therapy, but popular resentment has recently caused the introduction of less sweeping measures. From the beginning, Hungary has generally followed the more cautious gradualist approach.

Whichever route is taken, the move to the market is the accepted strategy for economic change. The economic revolution is, however, just one of the many revolutions taking place in Eastern Europe. There are also political, national, social, moral, ideological, cultural, and psychological revolutions swirling around at the same time. If economics could have been separated from the mainstream, unaffected by its other elements, then the building of democracy's material foundation would have been much simpler. All these other elements, however, have crowded in on it, jostling for priority, impeding its program, thereby delaying, perhaps in some cases even destroying, its chances for success. The postcommunist revolutions simply could not be an ordered or an orderly process.

Ideally, what the Eastern European countries needed was for their economic strategies to have had two years' unthreatened chance to work. After that, unfettered political pluralism could have been introduced with the real possibility that, with their economic bases ensured, they could then evolve into viable liberal democracies. Similarly, a measure of economic success might have assuaged, although never removed, the nationalist furies that have reemerged in parts of Eastern Europe.

Such a period of grace, out of the question now, still looked possible until early 1990 in Poland and until a few months later in Czechoslovakia. In Poland a genuine, democratic national consensus existed, based on the Solidarity myth. It might have ushered in, and steered through, the economic transformation, guarding it against the social upheavals that went with it. (It must be emphasized that it is democratic consensus that is meant here, not the martial law, or state of emergency, solutions advocated by some in the former Soviet Union and partly practiced in China.) Perhaps it was always too frail, even in Poland, to withstand the rigors of postcommunist politics but it was in any case deliberately broken by Lech Wałęsa, who had been its most crucial part, ostensibly in the name of "political pluralism." But political pluralism inevitably becomes (in the current Eastern European context) a political struggle in which the competing sides seek advantage from the social hardships the economic changes inflict. This is particularly the case where the shock-therapy variant is applied. Since achieving his ambition of becoming president, Wałęsa has used his charisma to try to rebuild a new consensus. But, once destroyed, the old Solidarity consensus, which, with Wałęsa driving it, might have been good for another couple of years, could not be put together again.

In Czechoslovakia the situation was somewhat similar. Civic Forum, led by Václav Havel, with his huge national and international reputation, at first looked as if it might do what Solidarity in Poland seemed set to do. But Civic Forum was never more than a pale shadow of Solidarity. Havel never gave it the political leadership it needed, and its brittle unity soon cracked under the pressures of competing personalities and political tendencies. (Thanks to the splits in Civic Forum and its Slovak counterpart, the Communist party is now the biggest single party in the Czechoslovak federal parliament.) Even more important—and in contrast to Poland—the Czechoslovak situation became complicated by re-emerging nationalism. Slovak nationalism began threatening not only Czechoslovak economic recovery, but also the very existence of Czechoslovakia. Even moderate Slovak nationalists began insisting that settling Slovakia's future get priority over economic recovery, which, in any case, they argued must be tailored to Slovakia's particular needs.

If nationalism has complicated the situation in Czechoslovakia, in Yugoslavia it has destroyed both the economy and the state. There, the federal prime minister, Ante Marković, prescribed in 1989 a reform course containing many features of the Polish shock-therapy treatment. Initially, it showed encouraging signs but was then undermined by a mixture of national antagonisms and retrograde politics. Five years earlier, it might have had a chance, but by 1990 Yugoslavia had already condemned itself to death; by the end of 1991 it had carried out the sentence on itself.

It remains to be seen whether Wałęsa can overcome the divisions he exploited in Polish public life and steer Poland to political and economic success, but it is looking more and more doubtful. For the moment it is Hungary that appears to most observers to have hit upon the most effective interaction between economic remedy and political cohesion. The enactment of the government's gradualist economic program, though not without controversy, is made easier by a concurrence among the main parliamentary groups over the need for basic change and in support for the new democratic system. Here Hungary benefits from its Kadarite inheritance—a quarter of a century of economic experiment (however fitful) and tempered authoritarianism. Hungary's main opposition parties regard the government's economic program as too timid, preferring the boldness of Poland's erstwhile shock therapy. By their responsible, consensus-building behavior—also a characteristic of the Socialist (former Communist) party—they have helped make Hungarian politics something of a model throughout Eastern Europe. Hungary's relatively promising economic progress is by no means unconnected with its stable political background.

In Hungary, as in the rest of Eastern Europe, looming doubt remains over eventual worker response to the social consequences of the painful transitions. For, everywhere, the worst is yet to come. Even in Hungary the taxi and truck drivers' strike in autumn 1990, though a far cry from the general strike some had feared, seriously jarred the public's nerves. It should also have been a reminder that industrial conflict can only be mitigated if labor's interests are represented more directly in the political process. Initially, in Poland the workers were an integral part of the Solidarity consensus. Now they are in political limbo. In the parliamentary elections in October 1991 many of them voted for either the far left or the far right parties. The Hungarian workers could eventually do the same. In Czechoslovakia, many workers, their relative well-being threatened, could drift back toward the still considerable Communist party, despite the fact that it has made less of an attempt than its counterparts elsewhere to shed its old, unregenerate skin. The early strong worker support for the National Salvation Front in Romania has now perceptibly weakened, without transferring to any of the opposition parties. In Bulgaria the bulk of labor is so far demonstratively for democratic politics and market economics, but its loyalties will be tested once the workers realize the pain economic reform entails.

There is real cause for concern here. For economists, of course, life would be much simpler without the workers, and the success of their efforts much swifter. The problem is to get the workers involved without diluting the reforms too much in doing so. Unless it is solved, or at least addressed, a key section of society could become an active obstacle to progress, even to the point of deflecting the move to the market economy.

If misgivings emerge about Western economics, then what about Western politics? Could they also receive critical scrutiny? Not yet—for several reasons. The memory of communist absolutism is still too painful for most Eastern Europeans to worry about the defects of the principal alternative. Liberal democracy is also a slippery entity, less tangible (and less initially painful) than liberal economics, and therefore less open to precise criticism. There is also much confusion about what liberal democracy really is. Many just identify it with anticommunism, the difference between good and evil. Others, a little less Manichean, confuse it with the political pluralism already prevailing, an error Milovan Djilas, the once stalwart Yugoslav communist and now communism's sharpest critic, and others have recently condemned. Only a few realize that liberal democracy is an end, a state of grace never actually reached (not even in the West), but eminently worth grasping for. These same few know that liberal economics is simply a means (perhaps not the only one) to try to reach that end. The means and the end may eventually coexist, even be complementary, but they can never be comparable because one is secondary to the other.

Devotion to, or perhaps mere genuflection toward, liberal democracy persists. But—and this is a measure of a certain disillusion—Western voices are heard suggesting that Eastern Europe, or perhaps parts of it, might need to submit to a form of interim authoritarianism "to get the job done," or, in other words, get over the worst of the economic transformation. It must, of course, be mild, enlightened, and definitely *pro-tem.* It must also not replace but function through the newly established democratic forms and procedures.

The case is arguable, but it is not ultimately convincing. The idea could also be dangerous. There is little in the history of Eastern Europe that guarantees that a "mild" authoritarianism could be kept from becoming something less than mild. The great political danger in Eastern Europe today is, first, a lapse into anarchy and, then, the rescue coming, not from any resurgent Left (at least not yet), but from a returning populist-nationalist-obscurantist Right, or from a military or a military-directed puppet government claiming to defend democracy while steadily eroding it. Nor is this danger solely confined to the politically immature and pauperized Balkans: it could also overtake the stronger polities of East-Central Europe.

What Eastern Europe needs today is not authoritarianism, but strong leadership both dedicated to and curbed by democracy. A look at the leadership lists is not reassuring. Wałęsa might lead Poland out of the morass that threatened during the presidential election in 1990 and returned dangerously after the parliamentary elections the next year, a morass for which he was largely responsible. He might also do this without using the authoritarian methods to which he is so predisposed. But confidence in his ability to do so decreases with almost every word he utters. Elsewhere there are personalities in plenty, but few who bode well as effective political leaders. Václav Havel's moral grandeur makes politics look demeaning, but that is part of Czechoslovakia's trouble. Prague's other outstanding public personality, Václav Klaus, although obviously able, has an abrasive, divisive public persona in a country that needs all the cohesion it can get.

Elsewhere, President Zheliu Zhelev does give Bulgaria a degree of cohesion and the Hungarian prime minister, József Antall, carries a certain *gravitas*. But the leadership in Romania is decidedly suspect, while the kind of leadership personified until recently by Vladimir Meciar in Slovakia, and still by the likes of Franjo Tudjman and Slobodan Milosevic in the ruins of Yugoslavia is decidedly dangerous. The brand of mild authoritarianism practiced by Thomas Masaryk, with his "presidential democracy," in prewar Czechoslovakia would be more than bearable in Eastern Europe today. But Masaryk was *sui generis*. (In any case his concept of Czechoslovakia was not only unsustainable but, in its "Czechoslovakist" negation of Slovak distinctiveness, downright destructive.) One consolation—a big one—is that now there are no external predators like Nazi Germany, Fascist Italy, and Soviet Russia, at least for the foreseeable future. This at least makes East-Central Europe safer for the muddled democracies and the creaking economies it is most likely to get.

OVERCOMING THE PAST

The Germans after 1945 called it *Vergangenheitsbewältigung*—overcoming the past. In Eastern Europe the same problem is so far nameless, but it still exists. It is more difficult and poignant than in postwar Germany. There, after all, the vast majority of Germans had supported the Nazis. The vast majority of East Europeans did not support their communist rulers, but they were brought together with them in many direct and indirect ways. The relationship was much longer and more complex than that in Nazi Germany. After six years of Hitler, Germany was at war; another six years and Hitler was gone. The communist system in Eastern Europe lasted over forty years and looked as if it would go on indefinitely, perhaps forever. Pressures for compromise and accommodation multiplied. Then, in an often effortless sequence, followed cooperation, collaboration, and coopting. Even in Poland, where communist rule was thinnest and most contested, there were over three million Communist party members—one in ten of the adult population—in 1980.

Such a tangled web hardly lends itself to dissection and categorization. Once the connection is cut the separate strands give no idea of the complexity of the whole. With this disclaimer, however, one can identify several aspects that are central to the issue.

First are those aspects relating to individual impact, response, and behavior. Transcending all of them is what Václav Havel has called "moral pollution": the duplicity, deceit, hypocrisy, pretense, evasiveness, and betrayal that sheer survival under communism often necessitated. The insulation of the real self, to which many resorted, also induced an apathy that has carried over to the present. In the political context this is most apparent in Poland and Hungary (although the calibrated nature of their revolutions may also be responsible for the miserable electoral turnouts since 1989). More universally evident is the lack of work ethic bred of forty years' socialist construction. This, though, could probably be righted quickly if appropriate material incentives appear. The habitual political language also needs shedding, not only the Marxist-Leninist gobbledy-gook (that is easily shed) but the mode of political discourse reflecting the deep "us" versus "them" cleavages in society which communism inherited and solidified.

Second are those aspects directly affecting the public realm. One concerns the future of the former communist bureaucracy, the legions of officeholders who sustained the system while it lasted. The strident demands in every country for their complete removal are now being accompanied by specific legislation to ensure it. The survival of so many of these placemen two years after the system was overthrown offends many citizens, including those who recognize the need for fairness in judgment and accept that prudent restraint in the weeding-out process will both help the transition to democracy and heal society's wounds. There is much emotion raging around the issue. Certainly, the protean adaptability of

some former communist luminaries is both impressive and gall-
ing. (Their lightning conversion from Moscow-dogmatism to Man-
chester-liberalism inspired the sardonic fancy about a traffic jam
forming on the road to Damascus.) At the end of 1991 what looked
like an extensive weeding-out process appeared to have begun in
Hungary, Czechoslovakia, and Poland. It was unquestionably popular and made good politics. There was also a need for more
rigorous screening than had at first seemed necessary, but it would
mean losing many able people post-communist Eastern Europe
desperately needed. It also meant more divisiveness in societies
already divided and it gave rise to unrelenting demagogy. More
importantly, there was the danger that the very foundations of the
new societies in Eastern Europe would be built not on legality but
on vengeful emotions, not on fairness but on injustice.

The old bureaucracy is one thing, however touchy; the old
security apparatus is quite another. Except in Romania, where
many of its members still lurk in the shadow or even strut in the
arrogance of power, the secret police—*pace* much public opinion to
the contrary—have been largely neutralized. It is not their present
impotence, but their past skulduggery that is at issue—and not so
much their own conduct, which is pretty well known, but that of
their erstwhile collaborators. Who did collaborate with them and—
a deeper question entirely—what constituted collaboration? As
the files have been opened, prominent politicians in the new
Czechoslovakia and Bulgaria—not to mention the old GDR—have
already had their careers destroyed. Many more could suffer the
same fate. There can be little sympathy for some; for others understanding and compassion should temper condemnation; still
others have probably been wrongly accused. Here, too, there are
possibilities for divisive demagogy, but also for sheer malevolence
and for tragedy. This is another issue that could vitiate the work-
ings of public life in Eastern Europe for years to come. Open the
files or shred them? Honest men can differ.

Finally, there is the issue of the restitution of private property
appropriated under communism—a matter of the past calculated

to rage well into the future. This complex, contentious issue burst onto the political stage in 1990. Again, it divides rather than unites society. In Hungary it threatened to bring down the ruling coalition government. Debate has raged about who and what should be compensated, how much, and from when. Many argue that loss of property should not be the only criterion for compensation. How many more East Europeans lost actual or possible careers through communism? How many lives were just blighted? Why no compensation for them? In more practical terms, the issue has immensely complicated the process of privatization, one of the essentials for economic recovery. But the principle of restitution has now been accepted throughout Eastern Europe and implementation is proceeding. Only the lawyers will derive full compensation from it.

NATIONALISM AND REGIONAL RELATIONS

When skeptics say the future of Eastern Europe is its past, they are referring to the reemergence of nationalism, not so much to the fact as to the force of it.

Nationalism was never fully submerged by communism. The Yugoslav Communists, seemingly the embodiment of internationalism, invoked nationalism in their split with Moscow in 1948. Nationalism was also a thread running through all the subsequent upheavals in East European communist history, from 1956 through 1989. In the interval, the special character of each East European nation continued unremittingly to cast communism in its own mold. Communism, supposed to make nationalism irrelevant, found itself being shaped, often warped, by something stronger.

All communism, in some degree, became national communism. But Soviet domination at least froze most of the violence out of Eastern Europe's national and ethnic antagonisms. They did not disappear; nor did their most vicious manifestation: anti-Semitism. But when both Soviet and communist rule melted, all the nationalisms, consequential or petty, resurfaced intact (as did anti-Semitism). They were partly, of course, directed against Soviet Russia, but they also circulated vigorously among the East Europeans themselves, not only across borders but also inside them, against fellow citizens of a different nation.

Eastern Europe's new leaders, and many of its citizens, realize the dangers of this situation and are resisting them. With some success they are urging cooperation rather than confrontation, within the region itself and with countries of Western Europe. Poland, Czechoslovakia, and Hungary are a case in point—the "triple alliance," as some have rather prematurely dubbed their association. So is the "Pentagonale" association, originally involving Italy, Austria, Yugoslavia, Hungary, and Czechoslovakia. The addition of Poland turned the Pentagonale into the "Hexagonale," but then the loss of Yugoslavia and the subsequent accession of Croatia and Slovenia threatened to bring about the "Heptagonale" and with it the suggestion of a numbers game. The new, safer title is the Central European Initiative.

These endeavors contain hope for a peaceful Eastern Europe, one that can proceed with economic and political reconstruction. Throughout the region, however, there is also a countertrend: a restlessness both feeding on, and feeding, the prevailing uncertainty. Within a period of a few months in 1989 the entire post–World War II structure in Eastern Europe fell apart: communist rule; Soviet domination; the division of Germany; the GDR itself; the Eastern alliance system; the entire Cold War. Not only that, but very soon, two of the most important new states emerging from World War I, the Soviet Union and Yugoslavia, began a rapid process of disintegration. To many it must have seemed not merely a case of history returning, but of the whole of the twentieth century being up for grabs. This being so, need anything be untouchable anymore: Trianon; the integrity of Czechoslovakia; borders in the Balkans; bits and pieces of the former Soviet Union?

Economic failure and political frustration go hand in hand with such hankering restlessness. They posit a dangerous situation. It goes without saying that genuine national grievances continue to exist. But, if East Europeans cannot create the conditions for their eventual peaceful redress, they will have betrayed the hopes of 1989. At present all their new leaders, minus a few in Yugoslavia, are resisting nationalist temptations. But they will need to be sustained in their restraint, both domestically and from outside. No one summarized the danger better than Alija Izetbegovic, president of Bosnia-Hercegovina, in an interview given at the end of 1990: "When you call for a public meeting about democracy, a couple of hundred intellectuals come. When it's about nationalism, you get tens of thousands of all sorts."

The number of "nationalist flashpoints," already burning or still only smoldering in Eastern Europe today is truly sobering. The following major issues have returned to the East European agenda: Czech-Slovak relations; Slovak-Hungarian relations; the Hungarian minority in Romania; Romanian-Hungarian relations over Transylvania; Bessarabia; Serbia-Croatia; the Albanian majority in Kosovo; Greater Albania; the future of Bosnia-Hercegovina, with its Muslim, Serb, and Croat communities; the whole Macedonian complex, domestic and international; Bulgaria-Turkey over the Turkish minority; the Greek-Turkish set of disputes, in which other parts of the Balkans could eventually be embroiled. To be added to this list (though it is tragically without international relevance or resonance so far) is the condition of the Gypsies everywhere.

Except in the case of Czech-Slovak relations where, come what may, a certain decorum will presumably prevail, all these issues— all relating to the Balkans—could explode into serious violence. In the former Yugoslavia they already have exploded: the raging war between Serbia and Croatia has abated, but may resume at any time. Serbia, a nation not without glory or grievance has recently behaved like a rogue elephant, rampaging in Croatia and threatening to career in several other directions as well. There is a whiff of 1912—the date of the first Balkan war—about the region, evocative and terrifying. History has certainly returned to the Balkans, especially those parts of it the nations there want to remember. In the

Balkans, as Robert D. Kaplan says, "History is not thought of as a chronological progression. It jumps around and moves in circles."

The great confrontation that could eventually overcome southeastern Europe will not be between Croats and Serbs, who are fellow Slavs, however antagonistic—that will be a relative sideshow. It would be further south, between Slavs and Muslims, Orthodox Christianity against Islam, stretching from Bosnia in the northwest down to Turkey in the southeast. (Greece, historically contemptuous of the "barbarian" Slavs, would inevitably be drawn in on their side against the perceived Muslim threat.) There are about 10 million Muslims in the Balkans (outside Turkey), of whom perhaps 1.5 million are of Turkish ethnic extraction. The Slavic Christian aversion to them is a compound of racial and religious hatred. It is evident today in Serbian, Macedonian, and Bulgarian attitudes. As for the Muslims, they have struggled from submission to a self-confidence bordering on militancy. The best example of this is in Bosnia-Hercegovina, which now boasts Europe's first Muslim president (the aforementioned Alija Izetbegovic) and in Kosovo, where Albanian resistance is growing despite Serbian repression.

Unless urgent regional and, above all, international efforts are made to head it off, this confrontation could become unstoppable well before the end of the century. If it occurs, it will probably not involve a general conflagration; rather an overarching tension punctuated by varying degrees of violence. It is hard to see how Turkey could stay aloof from such a confrontation. Rejected by Western Europe, the westernizing secularism of the Atatürk legacy giving way to an Islamic national introspection, the new Turkey of the twenty-first century might see itself as the ordained guardian of Balkan Muslims, renewing its involvement in a region it had formerly ruled for five centuries. The new Russia, however weak it initially may be, is certain to remain a major power, with national interests reflected in its foreign policy. The Balkan Slavs could again become a focus of its attention. In other words, it is not just history that would be returning to the Balkans, but also the Eastern Question, give or take one or two of its former principals.

INTERNATIONAL RELATIONS

To be accepted into, or back into, "Europe" has become, since 1989, not only an ambition but an obsession for most East Europeans, and not just East-Central Europeans: Romanians and Bulgarians also stress their once and future links with Europe. In the former Yugoslavia, Serbs and Macedonians claim to be as good Europeans as Slovenes and Croats. In Albania, too, all political groupings see Europe as the cherished goal, however distant.

The East Europeans want not just institutional acceptance into the EC and other organizations, but also general acceptance into what they see as the European heritage. Eastern Europe's aspiration toward this end constitutes an important, tangible factor in present international relations. It is partly, of course, a reaction against over forty years of Soviet Russian domination. That made many Eastern Europeans more Western than they had realized. Before World War II, a young Bulgarian going, say, to Berlin to study, was going to "Europe." (So was a Greek, for that matter.) Now, no one would see Europe in such distant, exotic terms. It is much more familiar and, hopefully, attainable.

No one yet knows how much this yearning for acceptance will be satisfied. Certainly, it is going to take longer than most Eastern Europeans realize. For the southeastern Europeans it may never be satisfied, and this could be as much Europe's loss as theirs. In practical terms, the Poles, Czechoslovaks, and Hungarians have started on the road to Brussels, a long road paved with frustration and disillusion, as well as good intentions. They will eventually get there. By the time they do, Europe, hopefully, will not have lost all its magic for them and become, as it has already for many Western Europeans, a technicality, a convenience, or an inevitability, rather than an ideal.

And yet, with all their current enthusiasm for Europe, the Eastern Europeans more than ever also want an American presence in their midst, an American commitment to their future. It is a question of security, in the fullest, most comprehensive, sense of the word. It is more psychological than physical, but no less tangible for that. Politically aware Eastern Europeans accept the fact that an American military guarantee—bilateral or through NATO—is still impossible (however desirable in the best of all worlds). What they want is linkage—a connection, informal, if need be, but perceptible—with the American-led alliance. They need this all the more as the unpredictability of the Soviet Union becomes increasingly plain. It has become trite (though no less true) to say that nowhere in the world does the United States enjoy more admiration and affection than in Eastern Europe. In more practical terms, Americans also enjoy the kind of credibility associated with power, and the successful use thereof, that the West Europeans simply do not enjoy. America's presence, and the assurance of its concern, are essential, therefore, for East European confidence in this crucial phase of their history.

The American role, of course, could never begin to equal the German role. East European feelings about Germany vary according to the historical relationship between Germany and each of the countries concerned. Many Czechs, Poles, and Serbs, especially the latter two, preserve their suspicions based on their treatment at the hands of Germans during the course of this century. In Slovakia, Hungary, Slovenia, Croatia, and Bulgaria there has been considerable popular pro-German sentiment, despite—in some cases, because of—the Nazi years. Romanians, traditionally pro-French but also fiercely anti-Russian and anti-Hungarian, have often been equivocal in their feelings. These historical attitudes have, to some degree, been carried over to the present. The equivocal attitude of the Mazowiecki government in Poland in 1990 toward Germany and German reunification was a reflection of Polish fears. Nor was Polish unease in any sense relieved by the Bonn government's initial hesitation about finally recognizing the Oder-

Neisse frontier, or by the militancy of part of the German minority in Poland. There was also considerable uneasiness in the Czech lands about German reunification. In more distant Serbia there was, it must be said, little sign of such unease until the Serb-Croat conflict had begun and Germany showed clear signs of siding with Croatia. Then the German "menace" became an overused weapon in Serbia's crude and self-defeating propaganda and diplomatic arsenals.

In the rest of Eastern Europe, German unification was welcomed, both in itself and as a counterweight to a weakening, but still powerful and unpredictable, Soviet Union. On the part of some there was a rush to curry favor with Bonn, not just for economic, but also for political reasons. German backing came in handy not only vis-à-vis the Soviets but also against other old enemies. What these countries worried about was not so much Germany's past role as its future commitment. They wanted Germany to be more, not less, active—a new *Ostpolitik* based on the revolutionary transformation that had taken place since 1989. Precisely at the moment of its triumphant reunification, however, Germany seemed to falter and lose the confidence it now needed more than ever. Three factors contributed to this faltering: difficulties in digesting the old GDR; dismay over Eastern Europe's own stumbling efforts at reconstruction; and the collapse of the Soviet Union.

More recently, however, the period of uncertainty appears to be ending. In both Western Europe, where it had often been accused of a lack of political will, and in Eastern Europe, Germany seems to be asserting itself and taking the lead. Bonn's initiative toward the end of 1991 in recognizing Slovenia and Croatia—regardless of the timing or even the wisdom of the move—has been welcomed by most East Europeans as evidence of a recovered activism based on realism. What they want now is for this activism to be reflected in greater economic assistance. There has been some fear, even in a traditionally pro-German country like Hungary, of Germans gobbling up the few sectors of their battered economies worth having. But it is not the kind of fear that makes them shrink from the opportunities beckoning. Even Poland concedes now that the "path to Europe lies through Germany" and some potentially promising parts of Czech industry have had no alternative but to accept German takeovers. And, after all, whatever the burden of the past, the new Germany is democratic, well-intentioned, well-situated, and well-heeled. Nobody can do the job that needs doing nearly as well as the Germans.

Yet, despite the huge benefits the Germans can bestow, there is a reluctance on the part of most of the new East European leaders to let Germany dominate entirely. This partly explains their enthusiasm for the EC: Mainly it reflects their aspirations to rejoin Europe, but it also means dodging the danger of having none but German eggs in their baskets. Even so, the EC, especially in its East European policy, really means little else but Germany. France seeks to resume its close relations with Romania in order to keep a foothold in Eastern Europe and, if Serbia's behavior had allowed it, would have favored the Serbs against the German-oriented Croats in the Yugoslav civil war. Neither France nor any other West European power—except perhaps Italy in the regions immediately across the Adriatic—has the weight that a meaningful presence in Eastern Europe entails. If it wished, the United States could undoubtedly assume such a presence, to some extent economically (an economic presence is essential as proof of its seriousness), but mainly politically and, in the broadest sense of the word, culturally, too. One thing America could do is profit from the enormous goodwill of most young East Europeans by instituting a massive scholarship and exchange program (public and private) that would bring the best and brightest of them to the United States for varying periods of experience and study. (One condition should be that they all agree to return to their native countries.) In this way America could influence the future governing cadres throughout the region to its own (and to their) benefit. The financial outlay involved is small; the political return would be substantial.

As Eastern Europe has tried to face up to realities in the West, it has also had to cope with what it had hoped, after the miracles of

1989, to be able to shake off: the continuing impact of the Soviet Union. Liberation from Moscow did not mean dissociation from it. Breaking away from the eastern grip did not leave Eastern Europe free to gravitate solely westward. Even when the Soviet Union still existed, visibly weakening and disintegrating, the problems of relating to it were immense. The old forms of the relationship, multilateral and bilateral, were dismantled and disentangled. It was a messy process, economically, politically, and legally, which was still going on when the Soviet Union suddenly ceased to exist at the end of 1991. Now, building the new relationship between the East European states and the successor states of the Soviet Union will involve grappling with issues just as important for their future as the ties they are forming with the West, and much more difficult.

One of the most crucial issues will be the immense, multilayered problem of economic relations. This would have been difficult enough had the Soviet Union survived, but now, with it gone, a new complexity has arisen that could take costly years to overcome. Russia will become the main economic partner for the different East European states and already several of them have rushed to sign economic agreements with the new government in Moscow. How reliable will the essential deliveries of energy and raw materials be? How sure a market will the new Russia and other members of the quickly cobbled Commonwealth be? In the next years the relationship will probably be less reliable than even the old collapsing Soviet Union was. If the economic situation in the new Commonwealth republics, at least in the short term, goes from bad to worse then the specter of mass emigration across Eastern Europe becomes a reality. There has been migration enough already to cause concern. A rivulet is one thing, a raging flood quite another. Eastern Europe, especially Poland, Czechoslovakia, and Hungary, could become a mass transit area, with Western Europe the ultimate goal of those pouring through it. Some apostles of doom in Hungary, a country specializing in the breed, are already referring to a new Tatar invasion—the twenty-first century becoming very like the thirteenth.

For four of the East European states—Poland, Czechoslovakia, Hungary, and Romania—the most important immediate consequence of the collapse of the Soviet Union is the emergence of independent Ukraine. Ukraine has now become a pivotal European country. Its relationship with Russia will obviously be crucial, but so will its relationship with these four East European countries, particularly with Poland. This relationship could decide whether Ukraine really enters the European mainstream. Together, these two countries make up a large landmass, considerable resources, and a population of over 90 million. If they cooperate they could importantly affect international relations on the whole of the continent, but if historical animosities between the two nations are allowed to prevail they could sour the future of the whole eastern part of it. There is a lot of *Vergangenheitsbewältigung* needed on the part of all the countries concerned now that Ukraine is free. If it can be done, and if Ukraine can come to working terms with Russia on its other flank, then the whole future of Eastern Europe will be profoundly altered—and for the good. If not, the hopes of 1989 will be dashed. Ukraine is that important.

CAN THEY COPE?

Agendas can impart pessimism. The East European agenda, after forty years of communist rule, can impart downright despair. It might be wrong, however, to see Eastern Europe's problems in terms of the classic Western counterpoise of hope and despair, success or failure. They can best be perceived in the spirit of William the Silent's famous admonition: "One need not hope in order to undertake; nor succeed in order to persevere." Life goes on regardless. In any case, there is no going back. Some of the reassuring basics of "real, existing socialism" may be missed; Czechoslovak workers may moan; and in Romania even minicults of Ceauşescu are sprouting from the disillusion. Putting George Orwell's *Animal Farm* into the new political context, nobody in Eastern Europe wants Jones back—at least not yet, and certainly not the way he used to behave. *Realpolitikers* in the West, mourning the brittle safety of the old order, should take note of this. So should Western ideologues busy penning their requiems for a lost Leninism.

Still, while not wanting to return to the past, many East Europeans continue to be disappointed with the present. There are many reasons for this disappointment. Some have been discussed earlier. The basic reason is that East Europeans have not yet recovered their characteristic patience after the incredible ease with which communism was finally overthrown. A system, a whole empire, and later the seat of empire itself collapsed with little or no warning. The ensuing exhilaration eclipsed the realism now necessary for the task of salvage and reconstruction. So much so that, as the immensity of the task has become evident and the uncertainty of this new, postcommunist phase in their history becomes all too palpable, many East Europeans react with disenchantment and skepticism. Only when the realism and patience that carried them through centuries of foreign domination return will East Europeans realize that recovery is no quick-fix, but the kind of drawn-out process with which their past has made them familiar.

The tasks of recovery are similar, but the chances of every East European country achieving it vary. Recovery here can be defined as attaining a stable, economically viable democracy—idiosyncratic, certainly, but along Western lines—within a generation. In general, the prospects for the East-Central European states—Poland, Czechoslovakia, Hungary, and, potentially, Slovenia—are much brighter than those of the South-East European states—Romania, Bulgaria, Albania, and those emerging from southern or war-torn Yugoslavia.

It is not just that the East-Central European states look better equipped for the tasks civically, politically, and economically. They are also benefiting far more from whatever Western concern is presently available—including security reassurances—than their Balkan counterparts. The East-Central Europeans may feel neglected; the South-East Europeans feel written off, noticed only when they begin spilling blood.

Obviously, though, favorable comparisons with the Balkans are cold comfort to the East-Central Europeans when faced with their own formidable tasks. On top of the problems they all have in common, each country also has problems peculiar to itself. In Poland it is the looming struggle between clerical Catholicism and liberalism. The one is Poland's historical driving force and the recent victor in the struggle against communism; the other is a relative newcomer to the Polish scene, but, in all its chaotic mix, now rapidly gathering strength. This could become a distracting, even crippling, struggle, with no real winner and Poland the only sure loser. Czechoslovakia is in danger of a new kind of dismemberment—self-dismemberment. The dangers to its integrity posed by Slovak nationalism are obvious. Any complacency deriving from the fact that most Slovaks at present do not want separation could be dangerous. In a deteriorating situation the determined pro-separatist minority could become decisive, especially as Czech interest in preserving the union diminishes. If separation occurs, the Czech lands would survive and could prosper—politically, economically, and culturally. Slovakia would survive but hardly prosper, and its democratic future would be in considerable doubt. In the meantime, East-Central European regional stability would have seriously suffered. Hungary, both politically and economically, looks to outsiders the best situated of all the East European countries, but to try to persuade Hungarians of this is a thankless task. This psychological nihilism could be dangerous, especially if the economy suffers a downturn. It could further encourage a self-pitying "Trianon complex"—the hankering after lands lost after World War I—to the detriment of the enterprising enthusiasm for Europe that still prevails. Slovenia, with a population of two million and not much history, could be useful and content as part of something bigger, but perhaps forlorn and coveted on its own.

However troubling some of these prospects may seem, collectively or separately, they are nothing compared with those faced in southeastern Europe. There, in all the countries, no matter how different in many respects they are, the Ottoman legacy, the Byzantine or Phanariot mindset, the Erastian tradition in church-state relations, overall pauperization, not to mention the communist legacy, form a desolate background against which to cope with the problems of twenty-first-century Europe. The impact of some of these factors can be exaggerated but they cannot be entirely overlooked.

The postcommunist elections held in 1990 provide a telling example of the lack of liberal political culture in the Balkans, as well as a sharp contrast with similar elections held in east-central Europe. In Poland, Hungary, Czechoslovakia, the late unlamented GDR, Slovenia, and Croatia, the erstwhile Communists, however much reformed or beguiling, were routed. In Serbia, Montenegro, Albania, Romania, and Bulgaria, they were all kept in power by impressive margins. (In Macedonia they would also have won, but the dreaded Albanian Muslim minority did so well in the first round of the elections that the voters gave the plurality to the extreme nationalist party—the evocative I.M.R.O.—in the second and final round.) The governing communist parties, of course, were much better organized. Besides, all the elections were marred by fraud, although they received a fairly clean bill of health from international observers and were, all in all, among the fairest elections ever conducted in any of these countries.

Even more telling and depressing than the results was the aftermath of these elections, the response to them and the subsequent counterresponse. Considerable numbers of urban youth, living proof of the distinction between anticommunism and democracy, responded to the election results with violence. This led to brutal counterviolence, often by recidivist "law and order" forces. In Bucharest, Belgrade, Sofia, and Shköder, violent clashes led to casualties. In Sofia the democratically elected Bulgarian government was ousted in November 1990 by a combination of parliamentary boycott, street demonstrations, and labor unrest. (It looked uncomfortably like Prague, February 1948, only in reverse.) In

Tirana something similar happened in June 1991. These, then, are the basic points to remember about the most recent political developments in the Balkans:

1. Reform, or former, Communists won the democratic elections;

2. Many anticommunists refused to accept the result;

3. Violence and repression ensued.

These points should particularly be remembered when attempts are made to portray the political juveniles on the postelection barricades as idealistic youth imbued with the spirit of Delacroix and consumed by the cleansing flame of anger. They are, in fact, one of the biggest threats to the development of a democratic way of life in southeastern Europe. (Bulgaria, it must be said, is emerging as something of an exception to these generalizations—an oasis, even, in a Balkan desert, politically relatively stable, with an economic reform in place—but its real test is still to come.)

An even greater concern is the nationalism—sometimes the racism and religious hatred—already referred to. The civil war in Yugoslavia seems to have convinced at least some of the doubters in Western Europe and even the United States that East European nationalism could have broader, dangerous ramifications. There is never any assurance that violence *anywhere* could be safely "fenced off." Trouble in Transylvania, for example, could affect Hungary, Slovakia, and parts of both the former Yugoslavia and the former Soviet Union. If Serbs refuse to live as minorities anywhere, Hungarians might start asking why they should too. Romanian irredentism in Moldavia could excite Hungarian irredentism in Transylvania. In fact all the *irredenta* that history has left lying around in Eastern Europe could spring virulently to life. Nobody could remain unaffected by this, not even Americans.

It is a situation demanding international concern, not only in the form of economic assistance but also of security arrangements. Efforts to stop the Yugoslav civil war have only shown how complicated the task is. The EC initiatives so far have failed. At the time of writing, the Vance mission, under the auspices of the United Nations, was finally able to arrange a cease-fire in Croatia in January 1992. In February it appeared that the way had been cleared for the deployment of a UN peacekeeping force, but serious violence could erupt in any number of hotspots throughout the former Yugoslav territory at any moment. The European Community was initially seriously disunited in its attitude to the problem, with Germany unilaterally declaring its intention to recognize Slovenia and Croatia and pulling its allies along with it. This was an early warning of how difficult any future united foreign policy is going to be. As for CSCE (Conference on Security and Cooperation in Europe), it has proved itself embarrassingly impotent on this issue. NATO has not been tried. But its writ can hardly be seen extending to southeastern Europe, anyway, although it does appear to be drawing the East Central European states—Poland, Czechoslovakia, and Hungary—into its protective cooperation. There would be a serious problem, though, if Czechoslovakia were to break up. Would an independent Slovakia be eligible for this cooperation? Also would Slovakia qualify for EC membership at the same time as the Czech lands?

What is needed is an international body that can mobilize firefighting forces quickly and effectively. NATO's spreading influence in East Central Europe might be a deterrent against resorts to violence there, but it is still no assurance against them. CSCE, conscious of its failure in Yugoslavia, agreed in early 1992 that it must move toward forming an armed component to cope with conflicts. The organizational obstacles to this goal still seem almost insuperable; CSCE is still only a grouping of states in the process of giving itself structure and coherence. With the recent addition of all eleven members of the new Commonwealth of Independent States formed from the greater part of the old Soviet Union, it has become, a different organization, with several of its new members clearly not European. This will take some digesting. In the meantime, it is hard to see CSCE achieving the effectiveness it needs and to which it aspires.

If the European Community develops along the lines agreed to at Maastricht, then it might, through the West European Union (WEU), be able to form the type of peacekeeping and peace-imposing force needed. In many respects this would be the most appropriate option, backing up the Community's strong economic influence with a commensurate military capacity. The WEU, however, is still taking shape, and it has yet to be decided whether it will be part of NATO or a European rival to it. For the moment, therefore, this leaves the UN. Cyrus Vance showed in Yugoslavia what could be done by skill, patience, and character. There is still much to be done to prevent the disintegration of Yugoslavia from spawning more violence. The worst may be yet to come. If peace could be imposed on Serbia and Croatia, then the credit and credibility that would accrue to the UN might enable it to summon up the means to deter and, if needed, restore peace to other conflicts as well.

The Balkans are by no means the only global trouble spot demanding UN action. Others, most notably the Middle East, might well take priority. This is why Europe must eventually take over the tending of its own troublesome flock, but "eventually" might be too late. The real question remains whether Western Europe, through the EC, can turn its developing inner unity into an outward-looking sense of responsibility for Eastern Europe as well, with the will and the means to do for the other half of Europe what it has done for itself. Even more to the point: Can it do it quickly enough?

2

AN ECONOMIC POLICY FOR THE UNITED STATES AND THE WEST

Robert D. Hormats

The countries of Eastern and Central Europe are in the midst of a number of dramatic transformations: from totalitarianism to democracy; from command and control economies to market economies; from forced participation in the Warsaw Pact and occupation by the Red Army to security arrangements based more on sovereign choice; from foreign economic relations centered on the Soviet Union to market-oriented economic ties with the European Community (EC) and the global trading system; and from underdevelopment to economic modernization.

Each of these transformations, when complete, promises a better life and a wider spectrum of opportunities for the citizens of the countries undertaking them—as well as greater stability and prosperity for the entire area. Each also presents a formidable challenge to the societies involved, and because all of these transformations are being undertaken simultaneously, the combined task is Herculean. The process is complicated further by the disintegration of the Soviet Union and the collapse of its economy—both of which pose enormous new uncertainties for the fledgling democracies and market economies of Eastern and Central Europe.

The United States is struggling to find ways to support these difficult transitions. It has responded in a more tentative and less forthcoming fashion than would have been expected from a country whose foreign policy was for so many years dedicated in large measure to securing freedom and democracy for Eastern and Central Europe. Its response has been governed in part by economic difficulties at home, a large and growing budget deficit, and a feeling among many citizens that the Cold War's end means that the country should channel more of its resources and energies into overcoming domestic problems. There is also widespread complacency about, and indifference to, developments in this region; many Americans believe that the United States is insulated by distance from the economic, political, and security repercussions of failure of current reform efforts in that region.

Greater U.S. attention to problems in this area is unlikely unless America's leaders are willing to underscore to their constituents how changes now underway in that area affect this country. They must explain that the political and economic reform process is important to this country for several reasons:

1. These nations have chosen to shed communism, thereby reconfirming the passion of the human spirit for freedom and dignity, a spirit embodied in American values and institutions.

2. Developments in these nations will have a profound effect on the future stability of Europe as a whole and on the future character of American relations with the nations of that continent.

3. The economic success of Eastern and Central Europe would boost prospects for American exports, for Europe's prosperity, and for growth in the global economy as a whole.

4. Progress in the area will improve economic prospects for countries of the new Commonwealth of Independent States by demonstrating that market-oriented policies can achieve positive results and by boosting their export prospects in markets close to or on their borders.

Although Eastern and Central Europe's economies are not as closely linked to the United States as to Western Europe, their prosperity will nonetheless benefit countless U.S. companies desirous of investing in and developing new export markets in the region. The nations of Eastern and Central Europe want U.S.

companies to become more involved in their economies, but many have been disappointed by lack of U.S. corporate investment. The more constructive and successful the U.S. government's role in fostering the transition to market systems and stable growth in the area, the greater the likelihood that U.S. companies will feel comfortable investing there and will be able to take advantage of growing commercial opportunities.

If the United States is to effectively support the political and economic reforms on which the countries of this area have embarked, American policy must stress several related themes:

- Economic reform in Eastern and Central Europe is a long-term process requiring a long-term American commitment of advice, resources, and patience.

- Although the primary initiative and fundamental political support for reform must continue to come from the nations of the region themselves, Western help is needed to support their efforts to mobilize domestic financial and human resources and to supplement them with outside technical and economic assistance.

- American assistance to Eastern and Central Europe should be exercised through bilateral programs where the United States can make a special contribution. In order to maximize the effectiveness of American and Western help as a whole the largest portion of aid should be channeled through multilateral institutions, whose resources and expertise should be fully mobilized in support of economic reform in the region and which can set consistent conditions for assistance.

- The United States should work especially closely with the EC, whose role in supporting reform in Eastern and Central Europe through trade, finance, technical assistance, and political encouragement is crucial.

- American business should be encouraged to assist, and to gain a foothold in, Eastern and Central Europe in order to take advantage of potential trade and commercial opportunities and to broaden Eastern and Central European commercial options.

THE CHALLENGE

Perhaps the greatest uncertainty in the transformation now underway in Eastern and Central Europe relates to the uneasy interrelationship between politics and economics. The economist's lag is the politician's nightmare. Nowhere is this truer than in Eastern and Central Europe today. Popular frustration with economic adversity—and indeed the initial impact of the very reforms needed ultimately to overcome it—is a serious threat to political stability. Democratic reforms have succeeded more rapidly than market reforms. Unless economic progress becomes palpable and widespread, democratic leaders who champion the market will face growing pressure to resign or alter their policies; prospects for civil disorder will rise.

Most citizens of Eastern and Central Europe are aware that prosperity cannot be achieved overnight. For a time, very difficult adjustment pains were being treated with stoicism, but patience is running low in many quarters. The longer it takes for living standards to improve, new jobs to be created, and inflation to abate, the greater the risk of political disarray. This in turn could lead to a resurgence of authoritarianism led not by former communists, who are largely discredited in the region, but by those who wave the flag of xenophobic nationalism. Already the political coalitions that restored democracy have become fragmented. This jeopardizes the critical mass of support needed for sustained economic reform. In Czechoslovakia, for instance, economic frustrations have exacerbated ethnic disputes of ancient vintage, which in turn further divert attention from economic reform and threaten the very fabric of the state.

Since 1989, democracy, characterized by intense political competition among individuals, interests and ideas, and energetic multiparty politics, has gained a foothold in much of the area. In contrast, marketization and economic liberalization—the pronounced goals of most newly elected democratic leaders—have developed more slowly. This difference in pace—which threatens the democratic process—has occurred in part because of a difference in the public perception of what is needed and what is possible in the economic reform process.

By now, the peoples of Eastern and Central Europe possess a general understanding of what a democracy is and how it works; the communist, totalitarian model has been rejected by large majorities in favor of parliamentary democracy. In contrast, not all of Eastern and Central Europe felt the same degree of economic pain or deprivation under communism, and not all economies there worked the same way. In Poland land was not nationalized, in Czechoslovakia everything was. The Czechoslovaks felt reasonably well-off economically compared to most of their neighbors, whereas most Poles, at least in 1989 and 1990, felt that their economy was such a disaster that radical reform was the only answer. Hungary proceeded down the path of reform and decentralization much earlier than others, while Czechoslovakia (except for a brief moment in 1968) experienced virtually no reform before the Velvet Revolution of 1989. So the determination to implement reforms, ideas about the type of reform required, and opinions on the pace of reform vary from nation to nation in the region, and within each nation as well.

There are differences as to how large and extensive a role government should ultimately play in Eastern and Central European economies and through what instruments it should exercise influence and authority. The U.S., German, Japanese, and Korean approaches to a market economy, among others, are being studied. Other questions include how and to what degree to privatize state enterprises and the level of social benefits—the breadth and height of the social safety net—that is appropriate during and after the current economic transition. In many nations the tradition of generous government social benefits cannot be disregarded totally, no matter how committed leaders are to the market, although the size and scope of such benefits can be reduced.

All of these questions have a critical political component. The transitions now underway will be extremely difficult. They need to be accomplished fast enough to avoid the inconsistencies and contradictions of an economy that must ultimately be driven by market forces in order to achieve maximum efficiency but in which the state retains significant powers. A company that buys its inputs at a market price but can only sell its goods at an artificially low, state-set price, or which needs to pare down its work force to become competitive but is prevented from doing so by state regulation, will find it difficult to stay in business.

In some cases, however, theoretically sound economic policies might have to be modified on the basis of ongoing experience in order to maintain a broad political consensus in favor of continuing the reform process. The implementation of complete and immediate price deregulation, while economically sound, might need to be tempered or phased in for certain items because of the adverse political impact of too sharp an increase in the price of staples. A high social safety net is required to assist the elderly with food and fuel subsidies and provide unemployment benefits to the many workers who lose their jobs during the transformation to the market, even though the budgetary cost might be high. Such measures probably will be required to ensure sufficient political support for the overall reform process; such support will be essential if that process is to be sustained over a period of years—as it must be if it is to succeed.

There is likely to be a difference in how citizens of nations living under legitimately elected and popularly supported governments respond to economic hardship and how those living under governments not enjoying popular legitimacy respond. Citizens of the former are likely to put up with more hardship for longer than those of the latter because the tough measures are being imposed by "their government" rather than a government whose legitimacy they challenge. In the latter circumstances, economic problems will be just one more reason to oppose the government in power.

A SNAPSHOT OF EASTERN AND CENTRAL EUROPEAN ECONOMIES

Despite variations in speed and intensity, the major characteristics of economic reform in the nations of Eastern and Central Europe are similar and their policy goals are basically congruent: greater reliance on the market, more private ownership, demonopolization, and diminished government control. A reform process based on these components inevitably inflicts temporary, in some cases prolonged, pain on the peoples of the reforming nation.

Even in the former East Germany, with all its advantages relative to the other former Soviet satellites, the transition to capitalism is proving difficult in human terms and more costly in financial terms than many experts had imagined. Since German monetary and economic union on July 1, 1990, production has fallen dramatically, unemployment has skyrocketed, and enterprises thought to be competitive and capable of earning hard currency with a little help from Western Germany are proving to be surprisingly weak. On the other hand, eastern Germany was the only Eastern European nation to *revalue* (up value) its currency. The decision to value the Ostmark at parity with the Deutschemark in order to stem migration to the western part of the country was probably the correct one given the alternatives, but it nonetheless led to a sharp increase in wage costs—which were also pushed up significantly by trade union pressures—as well as to a similarly sharp decrease in the price competitiveness of eastern German exports and thus to a collapse in the economic viability of many plants.

Despite these adversities, however, eastern Germany is making significant progress in establishing a thriving market economy which will both strengthen, and be strengthened by, the sound and stable economy of the western part of the country. Although western German funds are doubtless a critical element in promoting this progress, the underlying structural and legal reforms that support the market, large scale private investment, and massive technical assistance have also played critical roles.

Reforms in Poland, Hungary, and Czechoslovakia, on which this discussion will focus, are moving ahead, albeit less rapidly than their proponents had hoped. In contrast, Romania has found it difficult to create viable political structures and to reorganize the economy. Bulgaria has been slow off the mark because of political uncertainties, but it now appears to be on a steady and sensible course toward market reform. Yugoslavia, once an economic success story, has been preoccupied by the destructive civil war, which has crippled large parts of its economy, affecting even the most successful areas of the country such as Slovenia.

In all Eastern and Central European countries legal, political, and attitudinal hurdles to the market remain in varying degrees. They must be overcome if these nations are to be able to implement serious reforms. Moreover, the collapse of trade relations among countries of the former COMECON—and in particular between Eastern Europe and Central Europe on the one hand and the former Soviet Union on the other—has added greatly to problems of the region. For forty years these nations were tied together in a barter system in which market prices and comparative advantage played virtually no role. With the collapse of that system much uneconomic trade has stopped, but some commerce vital to the survival of certain enterprises which might have continued on the basis of market prices has also collapsed due to foreign exchange shortages and supply disruptions.

The demise of the COMECON system and the collapse of the Soviet economy, coupled with the disintegration of the Soviet state, have posed new problems for Eastern and Central Europe's reform process. The shares of exports from countries of that region to the Soviet Union in 1989 ranged from 21 percent for Yugoslavia to 66 percent for Bulgaria, and the shares going to other COMECON countries as a whole ranged from 34 percent for Yugoslavia to 83 percent for Bulgaria. Export volumes of former COMECON countries to other former COMECON countries dropped by 20 to 30 percent in 1990. This collapse inflicted a heavy blow on economic activity in all countries of the area. In 1991 the trade situation worsened further; for the first six months Eastern and Central Europe's commerce with the Soviet Union fell 50 percent below the comparable period in 1990.

The legacy of a deteriorating communist system, the initial phases of domestic economic reform, the collapse of the Soviet economy, and the deterioration of intra-COMECON trade led to sharply higher prices and increased unemployment throughout Eastern and Central Europe. Efforts to achieve greater economic efficiency and to force companies to operate without government subsidies in order to reduce the drain on budgets and bring prices to market levels, necessary objectives of reform, have meant that many antiquated factories have been or are likely to be closed and the workers let go. The point should be underscored that many of the closed factories, as elsewhere in Eastern and Central Europe, produced military items or heavy industrial equipment for which there is now little or no use. Declines in production therefore do not automatically translate into declines in the availability of goods to satisfy consumer needs; indeed, in most areas these have increased. The big impact of such declines is on job loss.

Also, heretofore controlled prices have been allowed to rise to levels that more closely reflect supply and demand. Privatization has reduced job security and led to elimination of subsidies that had permitted consumers to pay artificially low prices and enterprises to maintain bloated work forces. Sharply higher prices for Soviet oil imports, plus a decline in deliveries, imposed a heavy cost on Eastern and Central European economies in 1991 as did the fall in sales of goods to the Soviet Union and other COMECON nations. Overall, according to the UN Economic Commission for Europe, output in Eastern and Central Europe in 1991 was expected to drop by about 15 percent below the level of 1990, bringing output to roughly 25 percent of that of 1988; a further 16% drop is predicted for 1992.

A brief country-by-country analysis shows that considerable progress has been made in some areas while serious problems remain or are emerging in others:

Poland moved quickly to undertake bold price and currency reforms, expose the economy to international competition, establish an independent central bank, and privatize large numbers of government-owned industries. Unemployment surged as inefficient factories were shut down; it is now 11 percent and predicted to reach 17 to 19 percent by the end of 1992.

Inflation shot up to between 30 and 40 percent per year but is now abating. The country is enjoying a trade surplus as exports to the West have grown substantially. Goods are in the shops and new signs of entrepreneurship—if only among small traders and shopkeepers—are visible. Poland's innovative plan to privatize many state enterprises by placing them in the hands of twenty newly created investment funds and providing a share in each fund to every adult citizen should bring capitalism closer to the average Pole.

Benefits are not coming soon enough to satisfy expectations, however. Poles still see conditions deteriorating, must pay high prices for food and other items, are able to obtain fewer benefits from government, and face enormous uncertainties about future employment. Moreover, large budget deficits threaten price stability; these could become much larger still if recent decisions to raise pensions for many state sector employees are implemented. An excessively large budget in turn could lead the International Monetary Fund (IMF) to suspend support for Poland; that could jeopardize the 1991 agreement to forgive half of the nation's $45 billion debt, which depends on IMF support.

Having been brought up under communism to believe that government would provide an adequate, if only minimal, level of sustenance and economic security, many Poles were ill-prepared for the painful economic changes that reform has brought. Elections in the fall of 1991 demonstrated popular frustration—in some cases deep resentment—with the course of economic events and a yearning in some quarters for a slower pace of reform as well as a greater role for government in protecting the economic security of workers and pensioners. Similar sentiments echo throughout the region.

In Czechoslovakia there was less popular support for radical economic reform among the citizenry than in Poland; indeed many people felt themselves better off than their northern neighbors and felt that Polish-type reforms were not required. Nor was the country saddled with a large international debt. It did, however, seek as its highest priority price stability, and thus embarked on a major effort to tighten monetary and fiscal policy, hold down wage increases, and reduce the price-setting power of monopoly corporations.

Privatization has been an important goal of the government and in particular of Finance Minister Václav Klaus, whose commitment to the market is on a par with that of Milton Friedman. Enterprises are responsible for drafting their own privatization plans and can negotiate to be sold to domestic or foreign buyers outright, subject to government approval; small businesses are reserved for citizens. Seeing privatization as a way to demonopolize the economy, create a new kind of society based on widespread private ownership, and improve economic efficiency, Klaus has devised a unique program of creating vouchers that could be used to bid for stock in state-owned companies that are being privatized or in mutual funds that will purchase such shares. Difficulties include inadequate information for those seeking to bid on the companies for sale, thus leading to the risk of massive disappointment and insider advantage, and the sheer bureaucratic complexity of selling 1,700 companies so quickly.

Concerns about creating high levels of unemployment, and exacerbating ethnic problems between Czechs and Slovaks, discouraged the government from undertaking a large-scale closing of antiquated factories or slashing jobs in state enterprises overnight. Bold and imaginative reforms, however, are underway in many areas: price liberalization, big cuts in government subsidies, creation of a legal system that supports private sector development, limited internal currency convertibility to be followed by external convertibility, liberalization of the financial sector, reform of the tax system, promotion of foreign direct investment, and opening the economy to internal and foreign competition.

As in Poland, there is popular dissatisfaction with some aspects of economic reform. By not insisting that wages rise as rapidly as prices, however, the populace has permitted the country so far to avoid one-time price rises resulting from price liberalization (allowing formerly suppressed prices to find market levels) becoming embedded in the economy; that is, labor has not as yet demanded equivalently higher wages, which would again have pushed prices up, leading to an inflationary spiral. Whether this restraint is sustainable in the face of continued price increases will determine in large measure whether the nation's reform efforts will succeed. Also of concern is the large increase in unemployment due to a precipitous decline in industrial production, but, as in the case of Poland, much of the decline is in the state sector, part of which produced defense equipment. A fall in production in this area does not mean an equivalent fall in the availability of goods for the market.

Hungary began liberalizing its economy in the late 1960s. The process accelerated in 1988 when Miklos Nemeth came to power and a trade and cooperation agreement with the EC came into force. In 1989, company law was liberalized significantly, enhancing private business opportunities. In May 1989, Hungary became the first Eastern European country to privatize state enterprises. Current domestic economic policies encourage privatization through a program that aims to sell off 50 percent of state companies by the end of 1992 and the rest by the end of 1995; privatization can be initiated by management (the most frequent case), by the state, or by the investor—but the State Property Agency must approve all sales. Small business is reserved for domestic buyers and is being auctioned off to the highest bidder.

Price liberalization has been extensive. By the end of 1991 more than 90 percent of goods and services prices had been decontrolled. That corresponded to the liberalization of about 90 percent of the country's imports, which compete with about two-thirds of its industrial production. Trade with the West, up by 18 percent in 1990 and by an additional 30 percent in the first three quarters of 1991, has exceeded even the most optimistic expectations. Currently about 70 percent of Hungary's exports go to OECD countries.

Hungary has developed an attractive environment for foreign investors, who are permitted to fully repatriate profits and, if they own at least 20 percent of a Hungarian company, to receive a substantial tax rebate. Over two billion dollars was invested in Hungary in 1989 and 1990 and one and a half billion in 1991. Over two thousand joint ventures are in place. The policy of servicing the country's foreign debt is one of its highest priorities, as has been the effort to maintain a stable exchange rate to attract investment and hold down inflation. By 1991 the forint became de facto convertible for most transactions by the business sector and by foreign investors. The nation's interest and principal repayment obligations as a percentage of hard currency earnings dropped from 45 percent in 1990 to 30 percent in 1991 as exports picked up.

Inflation declined considerably from early to late 1991, although for the year as a whole it was over 30 percent. Economic growth, however, declined by about 9 percent in 1991, after a drop of 5 percent in 1990. Most of the decline, as in Poland and Czechoslovakia, can be attributed to a drop in production in state enterprises whereas output in private companies rose substantially. Despite the problems caused by the declining economy, support for the reform process appears to be relatively broad. There is little investable domestic capital, however, which makes much of the privatization effort dependent on foreign capital inflows, and there are underlying concerns about the deep recession in which the economy has recently been mired. Bankruptcies are likely to increase in 1992, and unemployment could rise to 20 percent of the labor force causing public disillusionment with government policy, although probably not with the overall movement toward a market economy.

In Bulgaria, Romania, and Yugoslavia political and economic uncertainty and turmoil have fed on one another. Bulgaria's political and economic crisis initially diverted attention from longer term, fundamental reform, but moves to the market and to attract foreign investment are now accelerating. Major goals include privatization of the state industrial sector, upgrading the banking system, revitalizing agriculture, and modernizing the nation's energy, transportation, and telecommunications systems.

Romania continues to experience political and social stress, but despite these has embarked on a bold privatization program featuring creation of joint-stock or limited-liability companies. Capital will be initially controlled by the state, but 30 percent of the shares will be distributed to employees, with the remaining 70 percent sold later to foreign or domestic investors. State subsidies in nonfood products were eliminated in November 1990. This led to big price increases followed by major strikes, resulting in high wage increases. Inflation rose to 20 percent in 1990 compared to 2 percent in 1989; in 1991 it shot up to 250 percent, with wages up by over 180 percent.

Yugoslavia had been one of Eastern Europe's great economic successes, but civil strife and the resultant economic destruction have disrupted progress. In 1990 the economic situation deteriorated significantly. The country was forced to seek an IMF standby agreement. In order to qualify, it agreed to make the dinar convertible and peg it to the Deutschemark, to impose a limited wage and price freeze, to institute rigorous controls on the money supply, and to reorganize the banking system. The former constituent republics have had their own economic policies for a number of years. Slovenia had been the most market-oriented; it had instituted measures to bring its tax regime up to Western European standards, to privatize 50 percent of all companies, and to grant tax relief to foreign investors. The civil war has taken a heavy toll in human lives, disrupted transportation, and lost production. The successor states will face a costly rebuilding process.

AMERICA'S INTERESTS

The United States has myriad interests in Eastern and Central Europe—and a range of compelling historic and moral obligations as well. The United States has reason to desire expeditious removal of the remaining Soviet (Russian) troops from Eastern and Central Europe and avoidance of any possible pretext in future years for interference by Russia, Ukraine, or other independent states of the former Soviet Union in the domestic politics of Eastern and Central Europe.

Further escalation of the civil war in Yugoslavia could lead to Russian political and military support for its traditional friends the Serbs. It could also mean German help for Croatia and Slovenia and French help for Serbia. Others could be drawn in as well. The Albanians of Kosovo will not remain forever still; they will be major players in developments in the region. The Hungarians of Vojvodina, too, are beginning to stir, evoking concern and sympathy in Budapest. The Macedonians, also anti-Serb, are rekindling nationalist passions in Bulgaria. Even in Turkey, which wishes to play a greater "European" role, there are voices favoring the "protection" of the large and growing Moslem populations in the Balkans. In short, that part of the world appears to be reverting to nineteenth-century habits. If the situation deteriorates further, Eastern and Central Europe, indeed the entire continent, including Russia, could not remain unaffected or passive.

Instability in Eastern and Central Europe caused by ethnic strife, economic discontent, or a volatile combination of the two, could spill over the borders of America's European allies. It is already prompting significant immigration into Western Europe, leading to higher social expenditures for maintaining and resettling refugees and strengthening nationalistic and xenophobic political parties in such countries as Germany and Austria. In Italy, the government was forced swiftly to expel relatively small numbers of Albanian boat people. Right-wing, neo-fascist groups have received attention and support in many European countries by campaigning against immigration on grounds that it undermines the "national identity" and jeopardizes workers' jobs. All of these trends could undermine the political balance in Western Europe and weaken moderate governments.

As leader of a growing commonwealth of democracies, the United States has a strong interest in seeing democratic ideals and institutions flourish in Eastern and Central Europe. Throughout the Cold War, that was a major objective of this country. Moreover, consolidation of democratic reforms would be a powerful new endorsement of the virtues and attractiveness of democracy as an organizing principle for national politics. It would be historic in its own right and strengthen democratic forces elsewhere in the world, particularly in the newly established independent states of the former Soviet Union, where democratic leaders are likely to come under greater pressure if economic conditions deteriorate further.

On the economic front, the United States has an interest in the expansion of market-oriented policies and principles in the region. The success of such policies, and the prosperity they should ultimately bring to the area, would boost America's own trade prospects by creating a growing market for its goods and services. Although relatively small compared to the Western European market, Eastern and Central Europe have the potential for extensive growth in coming years if nations there can overcome current economic difficulties. That would also provide U.S. companies a prosperous area in which to invest. Many American firms already see Eastern and Central Europe as a region in which to take advantage of low-cost, skilled workers to produce goods to sell in the vast and relatively high labor cost EC market. Ultimately their home markets will become more important.

The success of market reforms in Eastern and Central Europe also would help countries in other parts of the world—especially the sovereign states of the former Soviet Union—to gain confidence that they too can profit from adopting similar policies and institutions. They will be able to point to the experience of countries nearby to demonstrate to their peoples that the short-term pains of reform can lead to long-term benefits, and perhaps thereby sustain public support for such reforms a little longer.

America's moral obligations go to the heart of what this country stands for at home and in the world—the deepening and broadening of political pluralism and individual liberties. These interests and obligations confer major responsibilities on the United States. Its role in Eastern and Central Europe did not end when the Iron Curtain was torn down. That was just the beginning of what must be a process of sustained engagement, which must be particularly intense while the roots of democracy and free markets are struggling to take hold. The roughly two billion dollars in loans and grants to the region provided by the United States since 1989 is relatively small compared to its enormous needs and to the contributions other Western countries have made or the historic opportunity the United States has to achieve the consolidation of democracy and free markets in the region.

If U.S. interests in the area are strong, those of Western Europe are even stronger. It is upon Western Europe that history, proximity, and economic weight in the region have thrust the greatest responsibility for the future of Eastern and Central Europe. Western Europe has the most to gain from future trade if Eastern and Central Europe prosper; it also has the most to gain from the added measure of security that would result from stability in the region. Conversely it would be the most adversely affected by a failure of economic reform and by political instability in the area; potential effects would include a higher long-term aid burden, increased defense expenditures, greater environmental pollution, and unmanageable levels of immigration.

That Western European leaders recognize their central responsibility in the area has been demonstrated by the magnitude of their financial and technical assistance, which greatly exceeds that of the United States, as well as by the EC's willingness to move quickly to negotiate expanded Association Agreements that increase the access of products of Eastern and Central European nations to its market. In view of the EC's growing role in the region, it should be a fundamental tenet of American policy not only to work with Western Europe on issues relating to Eastern and Central Europe but also to accept the *leadership* of Western Europe on a large majority of East-West economic and political matters. That concept—simple as it sounds—was only established as U.S. policy at the Seven Nation Economic Summit of 1989 in Paris; there the EC was assigned, with U.S. support, responsibility for coordinating Western economic assistance to Eastern and Central Europe.

For much of the post–World War II period, the United States was accepted as leader of the West on most matters relating to Eastern Europe and the Soviet Union. In the 1990s Western Europe will assume the leadership role on many such issues. A number of the decisions of Western European nations, particularly Germany, regarding the nature of their economic and political ties with Eastern and Central Europe are already being taken with little reference to Washington. Many of these are being made in the context of the EC, which is increasingly the locus for overall European foreign and economic policy (but not security) coordination and policy harmonization vis-à-vis Eastern and Central Europe. This is so because, as in the case of Yugoslavia, Western Europe's greatest source of leverage is the ability to withhold or provide economic assistance.

The EC is the central economic institution in Europe today; closer trade and financial linkages to it—and ultimately membership in it—are the overriding external policy objectives for Eastern and Central European countries as well as for some of the now sovereign states of the former Soviet Union. It is appropriate for the United States to try to influence the EC as it shapes its policies and develops a new structure of relations with Eastern and Central Europe. The danger is that Western Europe will become increasingly preoccupied with constructing the 1993 Single Market, Economic and Monetary Union, European Political Union, and the European Economic Space (closer ties with nations of the European Free Trade Area), and thus become less willing to accommodate Washington's views as it formulates the new European architecture.

The single most important step toward strengthening democratic and market economy prospects in Eastern and Central Europe would be for the EC to substantially open its enormous market to agricultural and manufactured goods from the region. It has moved in this direction, but not to the degree that Eastern and Central Europeans have reason to expect, or that is necessary to significantly boost and reward their reforms. There are also worrisome "safeguards" that could be invoked to restrict sensitive Eastern and Central European exports to the EC should market penetration increase sharply. It should be borne in mind that the postwar German economic success was aided mightily by global demand created by the Korean War. Then as now supply-side reforms need strong demand to succeed. Large-scale demand for products from this region cannot come from within these nations because of their current efforts to maintain price stability and tight budget discipline; significant demand must come from their major trading partners—the nations of the EC.

The EC could also guarantee long-term borrowings by countries such as Hungary that reject a Polish-type debt rescheduling, just as it has done for EC members such as Greece. This guarantee could be conditioned on the recipient adhering to an IMF, or other, stabilization program. Interest payments on the loan could be collected for a few years in the loan recipient's local currency to minimize the hard currency debt service burden.

The EC also should be encouraged to extend full or, at a minimum, phased membership to Eastern and Central European nations when their reforms progress to the point that they qualify— with conditions for membership made clear early on in order to serve as targets for reformers. The very prospect of membership in the not too distant future—assuming agreed criteria are met—

would focus and energize reforms in Eastern and Central Europe much as it did in the recent past in Spain and Portugal. It could also extend the "patience" of citizens of nations in the region with the tough transformation measures they must endure.

The United States should not push the EC to admit these nations if they do not meet the necessary conditions. They would have difficulty adapting to the internal competition and complex structure of rules and regulations in the EC. Hasty admission could undermine the EC's own efforts to deepen its unity and to strengthen its prosperity; that would render the EC less able to assist Eastern and Central Europe and a less attractive market for that region's goods.

To emphasize the importance of the role of Eastern and Central Europe is not, however, to justify a minimalist American role. American interests argue for a sustained and extensive contribution to Eastern and Central Europe's multifaceted transformation and reconstruction process, especially in two areas:

- Augmenting the region's participation in the global trading system, by expanding opportunities for it to increase exports and urging it to broaden import competition in its domestic markets;

- Increasing financial support for reform in the region, helping it to mobilize domestic and foreign capital and encouraging it to develop regional solutions to critical energy, environmental, and infrastructure needs.

TRADE

Reorienting trade in Eastern and Central Europe away from heavy reliance on the former Soviet Union and toward the West (particularly the EC) is critical to the economic growth of the region. The success of companies in these nations both in exporting to market economies and selling in home markets where comparable imports are permitted will be a test of whether their prices and quality have attained internationally competitive levels. Commercial success in foreign markets will be necessary to earn vital foreign exchange; foreign investment alone is unlikely to be sufficient to permit these countries to import all the items they need from hard currency nations. Most of the yen, dollars, and deutschemarks required to finance such imports can only be obtained by exporting greater volumes and a higher and higher quality of goods to the West.

The process of increasing hard currency sales is well and vigorously underway in many countries. Between 1989 and 1991 Eastern and Central European exports to the West climbed by 31 percent. Polish and Hungarian exports of a wide range of manufactured and agricultural goods grew especially sharply during this period. Exports from Czechoslovakia were not far behind. A significant part of these export increases, understandably, went to Germany; but growth occurred in other Western markets as well.

These surges should not lead to complacency. Some of the large increases in exports are, of course, the result of genuine efforts by businesses in Eastern and Central Europe to develop new markets, keep prices competitive, and accommodate products to Western tastes, needs, and specifications. Hungary is a particularly good example of this; its entrepreneurs have been active in pursuing market opportunities abroad for pharmaceuticals and light manufactures. Part of this surge, however, also results from the sharp drop in demand in home markets and the collapse in exports to former COMECON neighbors; together these developments have freed up more goods for sale to the West. These increases also start from a low volume base, and further dramatic percentage increases will be hard to sustain. Moreover, Eastern and Central European countries must maintain price stability and competitiveness in order to continue to penetrate foreign markets.

The most effective Eastern and Central European efforts to export will come to little unless their products enjoy extensive access to foreign markets. Many steps have already been taken in the West to open markets to exports from this area: the EC has removed or reduced some discriminatory quotas (although, as already noted, there are good reasons for its going much further);

the United States has accorded Most Favored Nation (MFN) treatment to reforming Eastern and Central European nations. Western nations have also extended generalized preferences to countries in the region.

Important as all of these bilateral steps are, the Eastern and Central Europeans still need a more open world trading system in order to boost and broaden opportunities for their exports. Barriers to their textile, steel, and agricultural exports are particularly harmful. A successful Uruguay Round, which results in liberalization in these and other sectors, is vital to their economic future. Agriculture remains the most significant, but not the only, sticking point in these negotiations. To achieve a breakthrough the United States and other agricultural exporters will need to convince the EC to reduce sharply its agricultural import barriers and to cut its subsidies to the production and export of farm commodities.

Doing so would open new agricultural market opportunities in the EC and elsewhere in the world, in one of the few major product groups in which Eastern and Central European countries are currently competitive. Cuts in EC and U.S. agricultural export subsidies together would considerably reduce artificial competition for Eastern and Central European farm exports. There is a fundamental inconsistency between the West's preaching the virtues of the market and the need for the former communist countries to take courageous steps to implement market reform, and its own lack of courage in slashing barriers and eliminating subsidies that distort agricultural trade in order to permit greater agricultural competition in their home and world markets.

In these same trade talks the United States and EC also should insist that Eastern and Central European nations continue to open their own economies to imports. As reforms in these nations—price decontrol, reduced subsidies, privatization—take hold, their areas of comparative advantage will gradually be revealed. As a result, new, market-oriented trading patterns can be established.

The top trade priority of Eastern and Central European nations is to strengthen trade links with the EC and with other hard currency nations. They also have much to gain by trading with their neighbors in the former socialist world in product areas where trade makes market sense—just as it benefited Western European nations to expand intra–Western European trade forty years ago. To increase competition in their own home markets, which is necessary to contain inflation, as well as to participate effectively in the Uruguay Round, these nations will have to open their own markets increasingly to foreign goods by reducing quotas, liberalizing import regimes, and accepting one another's credit or currencies.

Because Eastern and Central Europeans currently lack export financing facilities similar to those of the U.S. Export-Import Bank, or comparable institutions in other major trading nations, some of its exports are placed at a competitive disadvantage. By lending these nations seed money to start such institutions, which should over time generate the resources to finance themselves and repay these loans, the West could help them to take advantage of market export opportunities. The terms of their export financing should be similar to those of OECD nations, to avoid subsidizing their exports with Western funds.

FINANCIAL SUPPORT

The lion's share of the financing for rebuilding the economies of Eastern and Central Europe must come from domestic savings. Although sophisticated capital equipment, new technologies, and some consumer goods must be imported, and will require foreign help to finance, a large part of what is needed to build new factories, reconstruct neglected infrastructure and clean up polluted areas involves land, labor, and relatively low-technology equipment. Cement, basic steel, and many types of machinery can be produced domestically.

Since World War II, most successful economic development programs have relied primarily on domestic savings rather than on imported capital. Spain's GNP in 1955 was similar to that of Albania today; between 1955 and 1990, it maintained an average annual savings rate of over 20 percent of GNP and relied on foreign capital flows, including direct investment and government borrowing, for no more than 10 percent of its total investment—no more than 2½ percent of its GNP. Finland, which in 1950 had an income level about the same as Poland today, saved between 25 percent and 30 percent of GNP in virtually every year thereafter, while foreign capital amounted to an even smaller portion of investment than in Spain. Most other successful economies have relied heavily on domestic savings to finance investment.

Eastern and Central European savings have been relatively high by international standards. The chief problem under communism was that they were inefficiently allocated; they were utilized according to bureaucratic whim or governmental plan rather than according to market standards of efficiency or profitability.

The need to rely heavily on domestic savings to finance new investment in Eastern and Central Europe puts a high premium on developing private sector financial institutions to mobilize private savings and to allocate such funds, on the basis of market forces, to productive investments.

Reforms in banking and finance are particularly important in this regard. Most Eastern and Central European governments have already reduced or eliminated the commercial roles of central banks—which under former regimes allocated credit to comply with the dictates of national plans. They have helped to create and given broad new commercial opportunities to private banks. Most also have removed the bulk of restrictions limiting the regional establishment of branches and the range of activities that banks can perform. In Poland, banks are now permitted to determine deposit and lending rates. In Hungary, interest rates were freed to find market levels. In Czechoslovakia, rates have been liberalized but not completely freed, because commercial banking is still highly monopolistic.

The IMF, the World Bank, the International Finance Corporation, the U.S. Treasury, and the U.S. Federal Reserve Bank all have played important roles in assisting financial reform in Eastern and Central Europe. Help also has been given to Poland, Hungary, and Czechoslovakia to develop stock markets. Many Western financial institutions have instituted training programs to develop the financial skills of Eastern and Central Europeans. The West must continue to assist these nations to build human expertise and establish institutional arrangements to mobilize and effectively allocate capital.

Help in implementing the privatization process by providing advice about preparing large companies for sale (through financial restructuring and improved efficiency) and effecting transactions beneficial to both sellers and buyers could improve and broaden the range of investment opportunities for domestic and foreign investors. Advice can be particularly useful in structuring offerings of such companies so that the funds raised are used to strengthen the enterprise rather than simply be channeled into the government budget. The goal should be, after all, to strengthen the productive sector of the economies of the region. Ensuring the necessary capital infusion and strong marketing, research, and technical assistance provisions in deals with foreign partners is an important way of doing so.

The recently created European Bank for Reconstruction and Development (EBRD) has devoted considerable attention to supporting private sector investment in the region, aiming to fund projects that underpin the market. It could usefully augment its efforts by providing loan guarantees to the region to finance urgently needed infrastructure development, which is important to build a thriving private economy. This is an area where funds are sorely lacking.

Nations of Eastern and Central Europe, despite their own best efforts to increase capital and savings, will have a significant and sustained requirement for imported capital. Large sums will be needed to develop modern telecommunications facilities, establish competitive new industries, and modernize existing plant and equipment by importing and adapting Western technologies.

So far the West has pledged about $45 billion to the region—roughly two-thirds is expected to come from multilateral institutions such as the IMF, World Bank, EBRD, and the EC. Only a modest portion of these funds has actually reached these nations. There are two major reasons for this. First there is a difference between nominal demand for capital and effective demand. Effective demand is the capacity of a nation to absorb and efficiently utilize funds. It normally is lower than nominal demand, which is the amount of a nation's request or desire for funds. The difference occurs because legal uncertainties, a paucity of well-developed investment projects, and the absence of basic business and financial skills limit the ability of nations to absorb foreign funds and reduce the enthusiasm of foreign investors.

The other reason is that disbursements of official assistance normally lag behind commitments, which customarily are drawn down over a period of years; in some cases net repayment of old debt to the IMF, World Bank, or other lenders has offset a part of new lending, while also reducing the attractiveness of investment in debtor country by potential foreign investors who fear currency devaluations and other problems similar to those experienced by Latin American debtors.

In contrast to the experience of Latin America in the 1970s, bank credit is unlikely to play a major role in financing Eastern and Central European growth and reconstruction. Banks, having been burned by overexposure to Third World debt, and in many Western countries (namely the United States and Japan) experiencing domestic problems, are reluctant to make large new commitments to the region. That means countries of the area will need to rely more heavily on direct investment and on portfolio investment in stocks and bonds. Their laws and policies must be conducive to generating large amounts of private investment by their citizens and from abroad if they are to realize sustained increases in growth and employment.

Foreign government support can make a big difference early in the reform process by helping startup entrepreneurs obtain the capital needed to launch or build the first stages of their businesses. The United States placed special emphasis on support for the Eastern and Central European private sector in negotiations on the charter of the EBRD. The Bulgarian, Czechoslovakian, Hungarian, and Polish Enterprise Funds established by the U.S. government provide modest but critical financing to fledgling businesses in these nations. Retired American businesspeople have also helped companies get started or restructure. The key to success will be the practical experience gained by Eastern and Central European managers and employees as they operate in a market environment.

The United States should support the leadership role by multilateral institutions in both financing and monitoring the process of reform. They, rather than individual Western nations, should set conditions for assistance in order to depoliticize conditionality and the monitoring process, and to avoid the United States, Germany, or any other nation from unilaterally becoming too deeply involved in pressing Eastern and Central European countries to take the painful steps that often are an integral part of reform. Multilateral institutions can also address another problem endemic in the region today; there are so many donors and consultants that it is often hard for recipient governments to sort out the advice they are given, the more so because it is often in conflict.

Nations of the region should be able to obtain advice from many sources and make their own judgments based thereon. The international community should also have a forum—for example the IMF or World Bank—for helping these nations to assess the impact of micro-advice on macroeconomic developments. For example, an individual nation might press a country to undertake a construction project that benefits its exporters by providing the initial capital on attractive terms, but the project should be scrutinized in a broader format to determine the impact of annual maintenance costs on the nation's budget and impact of debt service on its foreign exchange reserves.

As recently as 1988 the United States would have paid billions of dollars to bring about the collapse of communism in this region, a bargain price considering the resulting reduction in the threat to its security and thus the saving of hundreds of billions of defense dollars. Now, after the desired collapse, the region is no longer part of America's security concerns and must compete for economic resources along with other pressing economic needs in the United States.

Yet, if these nations retrogress because of their myriad economic problems, if they deteriorate into weak, nationalistic, ethnically divided, and constantly feuding states, they could become a source of enormous instability in the region—perhaps, in a worst case scenario, drawing in politically, if not militarily, their neighbors to the east (Russia) and west (Germany or, from a greater distance, the United States). At some point, nationalist forces in Russia or Ukraine could argue that instability in Eastern and Central Europe was a threat to their national security, and use that as a pretext for asserting their political (or military) influence in the area. Such instability, as one observer put it, could lead Europe "back to the future." It could also require the United States to maintain higher troop levels in Europe than currently envisaged.

Germany, more than any other nation, has demonstrated an understanding of the inherent dangers in this possible scenario. It is, therefore, supporting economic reform in the region with large sums of money and massive technical assistance. The Germans also recognize that economic collapse on their border would damage efforts to rebuild the five new states of the old GDR and to establish a zone of stability to their east. Moreover, the migration that could result would profoundly disrupt German society and weaken its economy. For much of Western Europe, migration from North Africa and nations to the east presents one of the most formidable challenges—some would say threats—of this decade.

Investment in reform and recovery in Eastern and Central Europe is one way to avert this in a humane way. It is far preferable to erecting new barriers—a new and ironic Iron Curtain or Berlin Wall imposed by the West.

The United States and Western Europe share a common interest both in averting turmoil in Eastern and Central Europe and not encouraging or forcing Germany to carry too heavy a political burden in the region or to play too prominent a role in monitoring reforms, which would make the German government and its neighbors uncomfortable. That is further reason for assigning the multilateral development institutions, as well as the European Community and the Group of 24, significant assistance roles.

A full scale Marshall Plan for the region is hardly feasible today, given current budgetary conditions in the United States and elsewhere in the West. The principles behind the plan, however, employing relatively small sums of money to produce major benefits by boosting confidence and forcing cooperation among recipient nations, could be useful. Like Marshall Plan assistance, foreign funds will only work if the recipients advance the process of market reform and eliminate the still extensive remnants of government control that exist in these nations. Better coordination of external assistance could make such conditions more explicit in Eastern and Central Europe. Germany, it should be recalled, received less Marshall Plan money than many of its western neighbors; its *Wirtschaftswunder,* while assisted by Marshall Plan aid, owes at least as much to the bold price, currency, and market reforms of Ludwig Erhart and his colleagues.

Drawing on another historical success, just as the European Coal and Steel Community led the process of Western European integration, so might creation of a European Energy and Environmental Community (EEEC) lead, or at least form a major component in, the process of integrating Eastern and Western Europe. Dutch prime minister Ruud Lubbers initiated in 1990 a process of strengthening European energy cooperation; that led to the signing in late 1991 of an Energy Charter, which includes Western and

Eastern Europe and the former Soviet republics. Signatories agreed to remove technical and regulatory barriers to trade in energy among themselves, coordinate energy policies, develop international energy trade, and ensure that energy policies develop in a way that protects the environment. The charter's first aim is to provide a pan-European market built on the principle of non-discrimination on the basis of nationality.

Although an ambitious undertaking, this exercise could have a substantial impact on Eastern and Central Europe by coordinating financing and technological help to enable these nations to increase domestic energy production and to obtain more supplies from the West. In so doing it would enable them to reduce reliance on increasingly questionable energy deliveries from the former Soviet Union and to close down dangerous and antiquated nuclear facilities, the Chernobyl-type meltdown of which could spread radioactivity throughout the entire region, including much of Western Europe. New energy relationships could be established between the EEEC and the states of the former Soviet Union to assist the latter in boosting oil and gas production in order to augment Europe's supplies.

An energy-environmental plan for the region as a whole makes economic sense. Projects included in that plan would be more likely to obtain private sector support than those that appeared ad hoc. Eastern, Central, and Western Europe are part of one "environmental zone"; Western Europe has a major interest in ensuring that Eastern and Central Europe can improve their environmental practices, so joint and complementary programs, backed by Western European and multilateral support, are both logical and necessary.

Another set of linkages relates to infrastructure. A modern telecommunications and transportation network in Eastern and Central Europe—connecting with Western Europe—will require substantial amounts of new investment. Most of this will only be available from the West. Many projects such as toll roads, railroad connections, and new phone systems can earn hard currency by carrying East-West traffic and are thus more likely to obtain financing if they are closely tied to Western European systems.

It also is in the West's interests to avoid a large buildup of unproductively used borrowing by Eastern and Central European nations in order to avert a Latin American–type debt situation. This will require an active exchange of information among banking and financial authorities of lending and borrowing countries with a clear system of warning signals to caution borrowers and lenders when debt levels threaten to become too high.

CONCLUSION

The United States retains significant interests in Eastern and Central Europe. The end of the Cold War should not mean the end of American commitment to democracy and market economies in the region. The region cannot be marginalized because of our preoccupation with developments in the former Soviet Union or budget stringency at home.

The United States must pursue its interests in conjunction with the EC—encouraging ultimate EC membership for nations whose economic reforms have advanced sufficiently to qualify for this step, closer Eastern and Central European trade ties with the EC and the market economies of the West, and development of new Eastern and Central European–Western European infrastructure projects.

There must also be a major effort to integrate these countries into the global economy in areas such as trade and finance. The United States should champion this process and augment programs of its own to sustain financial and technical assistance to nations of the region, helping them to work through the transitions now underway.

There are no shortcuts here. The process will require a long-term U.S. commitment—if not for the economic benefits of success for U.S. business then because of the improved security and political environment that will result from the region's prosperity and stability. Ultimately it is the moral and political authority of the United States as the leader of the democratic world that is being tested. If America fails to play a constructive and substantial role, both its claim to global leadership and its standing as leader of the free world will suffer.

3

HARMONIZING U.S. AND EUROPEAN INTERESTS

William H. Luers

The current political and economic transformation of the Eurasian continent will mark the most significant shift in the nature of the transatlantic relationship since World War II. Prior assumptions about the scope and shape of "Europe" are now being revised. As the cultural and geopolitical differences among European peoples reassert themselves, the very definition of Europe is undergoing change. As the great economic division between rich and poor forms a new curtain from the Elbe to the Adriatic, paralysis is setting in, inhibiting the recent movement toward a "Europe whole and free." Just as the interests of the new Eastern states are becoming more divergent, Europe's two historic great powers, Germany and Russia, are undergoing major shifts in their make-up, their policies, and in perceptions of their own national interests. The ambitious, united European Community (EC) is straining to sustain direction, and to fulfill the dreams that fueled its progress for two decades or more.

American interests in Europe have already become less well-defined and immediate. America's leadership role in Europe's political evolution is rapidly diminishing. The leverage or influence the United States can or should exercise in Europe will continue to be pivotal for individual European nations and on discrete issues, but its ability to shape the Europe of tomorrow is paltry compared to the role it played for decades after World War II.

The interests of the former Soviet Union are becoming more diffuse as the heirs to the former superpower reel under the triple impact of the end of communism, the collapse of empire, and the decentralization of politics and the economy. The obsession with internal transformation and economic decline in the great Slavic nations of the former Soviet Union will continue to be the core drama of the East. The revived aspirations of the peoples and nations of East-Central Europe will accelerate ferocious competition, strife, and instability in a region formerly held stable by Soviet power.

In sum, the next decade will see in Europe and in the "Atlantic Alliance" uncertainty and a reshuffling of political and economic structures and assumptions on a scale unimaginable today. This is not to suggest that instability will lead once again to major regional wars or another world conflagration. It is, however, likely that local unrest and civil war could combine with economic decline in the post-communist states to strain European common purpose and become a serious divisive factor within the Western alliance.

In such an environment, the countries of East-Central Europe are, as always, likely to be both the victims and protagonists of the instability. The problem with the nations of Eastern Europe is that they produce more history than they can consume locally. So it is likely to be again in the 1990s, as they emerge from a half century of political suppression and economic collapse under communism.

Harmonizing the changing interests of the various national groups of the new Europe is a formidable task. Can the United States, Russia, and the larger nations of Europe avoid making East-Central Europe, once again, the focus of new divisions and struggles that have characterized the past five hundred years of European history?

THE EUROPEAN COMMUNITY— PARTICULARLY GERMANY

The heart, the mind, and the prosperity of Europe will continue to reside in the few industrialized economies of Western Europe for the foreseeable future. Germany, France, England, Italy, and the Benelux presently define what it is to be European. The have-not nations are trying to shape themselves in that image—up to a point. The Iberian states (now insider countries) and the "western" East Europeans, such as Poland, Czechoslovakia, and Hungary (now outsiders), want to become highly functional, advanced industrial players like the West European role models. Joining the EC and its affiliates is the goal. Building political, legal, communications, transportation, and cultural institutions on the scale and operational efficiency of Western Europe will motivate the nations on the fringe to seek to become grafted onto the dynamic Western core.

The most powerful draw—the ultimate persuasion—for the poorest nations of Europe to become modern, democratic, free market states is the possibility of joining the EC elite. This is a powerful incentive for shaping the policies and the pace of development in both Eastern and Southern Europe, but there are multiple developments which undercut or counterbalance the strong Western pull. There are centrifugal forces within the EC itself which could well weaken the force of the magnet.

Germany, the power center on the continent, is subject to the most dramatic internal changes in national identity—and national interests—of any of the nations of Western Europe. As the front-line nation for forty years and the potential battleground of a cataclysmic war, the Germans adapted well to a pacific role. From being the penitent, divided, and ultimately the most supportive ally of the United States, Germany, almost overnight, has resumed its historic, oft-interrupted agenda: the integration of the many Germanies into one state; an accommodation with France's proverbially fractured sense of dignity; an unavoidably dominant role in Central and Eastern Europe; and the management of its historic attraction and repulsion relationship with Russia. While trying to rethink how to exercise their renewed central role, the Germans realize that the absorption of East Germany may take a decade or more, and cost well over one trillion dollars in the 1990s. Unification will also likely result in a significantly new distribution of political power within Germany, and stir up anxieties and uncertainties that have only been suggested in the debate over moving the capital back to Berlin.

The external factors that affect the dynamics of the EC have already demonstrated they will affect Germany more dramatically than the other members. The EC, after all, evolved under the optimum conditions of the Cold War. Its members were bonded by a common external enemy and by a supportive United States, which consistently placed the NATO alliance above all other considerations. Now this unifying pressure is off. Multiple nonsecurity issues are intruding on the EC agenda of "strengthening and deepening": immigration; nationalism; assistance to the Soviet Union and the other post-communist economies; peacekeeping in Yugoslavia and potentially elsewhere; the shape of new European political and security structures, sale of military, nuclear, and chemical weapons technology in the Third World; and the divisive issues of the form political "federalism" and monetary union might take. These mounting tensions are working against the strong thirty-year momentum toward greater unity, exemplified in the agreements signed by the European Community at Maastricht.

The migration issue demonstrates the problem most dramatically. Germany is the nation most attractive to European migrants, because of its dynamic economy and its central location. At the same time, Germany is the state traditionally most uncomfortable with the concept of a multicultural society that large-scale immigration would create. The emergence of the skinheads in Germany and other parts of Central Europe is only one superficial indicator of a growing set of tensions over the role of immigrants in society. Are the Germans prepared to adapt to the legal, political, and social implications of assimilating large bodies of German and non-German peoples in the new unified state?

Moreover, anticipating migration waves from the East, Germans are more likely than their EC partners to lavish economic assistance, investment, and political attention on the region as a whole in order to reduce the "push" factors contributing to the migration from the poorer countries. Note particular efforts to persuade the Russian republic to reestablish the German autonomous republic on the Volga, for which Germany will pay handsomely. The unwise, short-term wage and currency policies in the eastern part of Germany also were designed to head off migration westward. The historic German proclivity to extend their political and economic influence eastward will be reinforced by their practical desire to reduce migration from the East.

Should emigration from the East swell to unacceptable levels, the Germans are more likely than, say the French or Italians, to move toward stricter border and internal controls on immigration—and to be more effective in implementing them. At certain levels, as we know in the United States, such internal controls can rub up against the legal principles of a democratic state and the protection of human rights.

Nationalism in the East, combined with migration to the West, is also likely to stimulate nationalist reactions in the West. The competing aspirations and increasingly desperate economic straits of the Slavic nations in the East are already provoking diverse national reactions in the EC, certainly in Germany. Moreover, as nationalism incites local conflicts and civil wars, the question will be posed: who will keep the peace? Neither the EC nor the new Russian state seem very likely candidates. How far, then, can UN authority reach into civil wars that are beginning to look like national wars, as in the former Yugoslavia, in Nagorno-Karabak, and in Georgia (where it is both)?

The war in the former Yugoslavia goes directly to the point. In December 1991, Germany, after months of urging the recognition of Croatia and Slovenia as independent states in order to focus the world on the Serbian communist aggression, finally pressed the EC to recognize the two states. The German position was motivated by several factors:

1. Historic special ties to Slovenia and Croatia, most particularly during World War II when Croatia was a Nazi ally (which is one of the very factors that evoke strong Serbian feelings against the Croats);

2. The German judgment that the EC's failure to recognize Slovenia and Croatia was unjust and, most importantly, the belief that the policy of nonrecognition actually supported the Serbian military action and Belgrade's desire to create a Greater Serbia;

3. The belief that nation states are still the key actors in Europe, and that the politics of balance of power (for example, supporting and even arming the Croats and Slovenes so that they can defend themselves) are the best way to keep states from going to war.

The balance of power approach clearly runs counter to the view of the United States and some other Western states, which prefer UN and peacekeeping approaches, and are reluctant to promote further balkanization of the region.

The debate over whether to use a balance of power or a multinational peacekeeping approach represents both a conceptual and practical difference in approach that must be addressed not only in the former Yugoslavia but throughout the entire region, including the former Soviet Union. Arms build-up and the development of national military establishments in the new state entities could well create a situation similar to that of Latin America after World War II, where the only strong central force was the military which dominated Latin American politics for thirty years. Yet, if balance of power is not applied in the region, which external forces can or will keep the peace?

It is not surprising that Germany would have a more sympathetic understanding toward the new nationalism in the East than the other, older and more jaded nations of the EC. Germany is, after all, the youngest state—having achieved nationhood in the second half of the nineteenth century, and only in 1990 united once again. Germany's instinct, therefore, on how to manage nationalist enthusiasms in the East may well be more sympathetic than the reactions of other Western nations because German nationalism is so fresh. Moreover, the traditional dominant German role throughout the region gives them a wide margin on knowledge and experience in the terrain. It will not be surprising to see Germany using balance of power strategies as it looks eastward while working within international institutions in its Western dealings.

Germany's role will be an important component of Western policy toward the East. Other Western nations will have to work with Germany—often taking its lead—toward evolving an internationalist and cooperative approach (if German policy is consensual with the West). Other steps to reinforce Germany's sense of engagement in international cooperation will be the growth of EC institutions and, perhaps, Germany becoming a permanent member of the UN Security Council.

None of the foregoing is to suggest that the EC is on the road to disintegration or to a major setback in its drive toward economic unity. It does suggest, however, that many new factors are already reducing the degree to which the member states pursue common policies.

The overriding question in this environment of changing national interests is: To what extent can or should the policies and institutions that are now in place be adapted to incorporate the post-communist states into a broader European system? Will associated membership in the EC and membership in the less substantive organizations, such as the CSCE and the Council of Europe, be sufficient to motivate and assist the new post-communist states or will new structures and larger commitments of resources, time, and political attention be required? It seems clear that the institutions now in place, none of which were designed for such an expanded Europe, will either have to undergo substantial revision, be supplemented, or replaced by new institutions in this decade. Can the EC really widen and deepen at the same time? The chances are doubtful. Can the United States influence the EC on these issues? Perhaps, but only with greater skill and more subtle policies than we have recently demonstrated.

THE FORMER SOVIET UNION—PARTICULARLY RUSSIA

The most significant phenomenon of the 1990s will be generated by the successor states of the former Soviet superpower, as they grope for new roles in the world. The interests of the former Soviet empire emanate less and less from one central source of authority and power and increasingly reflect the diffusion of power among and within the republics. This situation has resulted in a power vacuum in the heart of the Eurasian continent. It also forces the countries that border on the former Soviet Union to redefine their own interests. It is impossible to predict what the former Soviet Union will look like in a year or two, much less toward the end of the decade. One can and should, however, take note of certain characteristics that might affect the rest of Europe and the United States.

If the Western European nation that has undergone the most dramatic change in the past two years is Germany, the transformation of the former Soviet Union has been the single most dramatic event perhaps in the modern history of the East, including the last two centuries of the tsars, and the Great October Revolution. Parts of the Russian-Soviet empire may for the first time pursue a genuine course of Westernization and modernization, but other parts will not.

Such simultaneous dramatic changes in Europe's two major powers will, by any measure, contribute to instability in Europe, indeed throughout the industrialized world. The democratic and economic evolution of the former Soviet Union, combined with the demise of communist ideology, offers hope that the present instability will not have significant military or security implications. That, however, is by no means certain.

What characteristics, then, of this disintegrating empire will affect the interests of the nations of the former Soviet empire toward Europe? First, the major power that has emerged from the disintegration of the Soviet Union is Russia. It will be difficult to take seriously the Commonwealth of Independent States, or whatever it turns into over time, as the individual states struggle with nationhood and identity. The Russia that is emerging will, out of necessity, continue to have economic relationships with and maintain substantial, and perhaps increasing, political influence over the lesser republics. Russia's size and control over vital resources almost ensure Russian efforts to dominate, just as history almost ensures the resistance of the smaller states to Russian authority.

The leaders of Russia will need a unifying definition or set of themes for this vast new state, which may prove to be ungovernable in itself. The main objective will be to cast aside the communist revolution and socialist ideal and seek to justify the holding together of the Russian core. Whether the new Russia evolves into a traditional, xenophobic Russian model or into a more Western, democratic form will remain a question for some time. It will probably have characteristics of both.

The new leadership of post-communist Russia will, of necessity, place high priority on enticing Western, Japanese, and Association of Southeast Asian Nations (ASEAN) investment and assistance to build their economy. This external priority is likely to be undercut by internal ethnic and regional strife or civil war, and by profound differences over the political form of the new state. The ghost of Lenin and the heritage of socialism are likely to remain embedded in the minds and behavior of Russians for decades. The non-Slavic republics of the former USSR will liberate themselves more swiftly from the dead hand of Marxism-Leninism, but liberating the Russian government and bureaucracy from the old habit of central authority will prove a far more difficult task.

One of the worst scenarios for the new state would be a new Russian authoritarianism that sought to purge the society of Lenin and of communism as the only way to move on to a new course. In doing so, the new regime could end up repeating the horrors of Stalinism. The most hopeful obstacle to a recidivist Russian terror directed from the center is the fact that Russian society today is experiencing a dramatic decentralization and diffusion of power—the beginnings of a true civil society.

It remains difficult, despite the hopeful developments under Gorbachev and since, to imagine the new Russian state soon becoming democratic. The combination of factors working against a Western form of democracy and free market economy is formidable. The only questions seem to be how bad things will become and how reactionary and aggressive the new authority might be. Russian history does not offer much comfort in this regard. The West and the nations of East-Central Europe will have to be alert to the dangers that a conservative Russian state might pose.

A second characteristic of the new Russian state is that it will be bordered by former allies or former Soviet republics in varying degrees of civil war and/or hostility toward the Russian state. Border disputes, ethnic tensions, and control over military capacity may overwhelm the agenda of economic development and institution-building:

- The Baltic states are seeking protection in Western ties; they will try to secure their eastern borders with Western support, while moving quickly to rid themselves of all vestiges of communist and Russian subjugation, even while retaining economic links with the Russian state.

- Moldava and Romania could become partners in one of the most troubled post-communist settings in Eastern Europe. The stability of post–World War II borders would be directly challenged if these two states unite. The large Russian/Ukrainian population of Moldava will resist a Greater Romanian state.

- The passionate Georgians and the desperate and isolated Armenians, with their ethnic wars with the Azeris, are likely to contribute to a long period of strife and instability in the Transcaucasus. Independence in this region is not likely to bring democracy or protection of minority rights. The entire Transcaucasus region could well become like the former Yugoslavia, a candidate for UN involvement, foreign intervention, or international indifference to prolonged violence and civil war.

- Eastern and western Ukraine and the Crimea will increasingly experience an unstable association with their neighbors, particularly Russia, while Poland becomes a powerful factor in the politics of bordering western Ukraine, Belarus, and Lithuania. Border disputes, religion, and ethnic minorities are becoming major sources of tension threatening the process of economic transformation.

- The independent Turkic republics of Central Asia— Uzbekistan, Kazakhstan, Kirghizstan, and Turkmenistan, plus Azerbaijan and the Persian Tadzhikistan, will seek to increase their leverage on Moscow. The geopolitics of Central Asia will mix with the rising attention to Islamic fundamentalism to undermine the historic ties of these republics to Russia.

We must begin to think of the former Soviet empire in a new way. Rather than thinking of it in terms of the nationalities of the former Soviet empire, we must begin to think of dozens of small nations with new regional alliances and local interactions—from the Eastern European border, along Turkey's border, to China and Japan—a vast empire turned inside out. A new, perhaps more open, and certainly more unstable, Eurasian land mass is the major byproduct of the collapse of the Soviet empire. Balance of power politics are already underway throughout this vast region with Asian, Middle Eastern, and European powers already choosing favorites for economic and political support, shaping alliances, and surely eventually providing military assistance and arms. Before long, the principal challenge to the government of the new Russian state will be whether to become directly involved politically and militarily in the regional turmoil.

The former Soviet satellites in Eastern Europe will, in the new Europe, both torment and be tormented by Russia; they will also interpret and be interpreted by Russia for the West. They will become tormentors as the allies of the new democrats among the small ethnic nationalities within the former Soviet empire. Slavic, religious, and border alliances will be revived, as borders of all types are fought over and redefined. They will be tormented by the residue of the former Soviet empire's network of authority, which is still embedded in Eastern Europe, and which could indulge in mischief to undermine the success and harmony of the new states of Europe.

They will also be interpreters, as western and southern Slavs explain and advise the West on how to deal with the eastern Slavs and the Great Russians. The western Slavs will want the eastern Slavs as part of Europe, though perhaps not at the expense of having Western Europe focus most of its attention on Russia. The East Europeans will also be interpreted by the Russians, who will continue to have better access to Western power, and seek advantage for themselves. Eventually, the Russians will try to reestablish influence, partly to counter that of Germany.

It would be ironic if, at the end of this century, Russia became once again, as at the end of the nineteenth century, locked into a joint effort with the other Slavic nations for respect and power-sharing in Europe. World War I was really the culmination of a Russian-supported Slavic effort throughout eastern and southern Europe to break with the Hapsburg and Turkish empires. If the "North-South border"—an equivalent of the Rio Grande—separating wealthy and secure Western Europe from the poor and struggling East becomes a new curtain dividing Europe, some of the Eastern states may find no better friend than a large and powerful Russia.

On the other extreme is the possibility that the West's economic and political concentration on salvaging Russia and the other former Soviet republics might leave the nations of East-Central Europe adrift once again. If there is one nightmare in Eastern Europe today, it is the possibility of another Munich deal at the end of this century, in which the future of these small nations is set by Europe's great powers—decisions taken "about us, without us."

A third characteristic of the new Russian state will likely be erratic behavior as it tries to accommodate the many internal and external challenges. The West has been conditioned to think of Soviet leaders as determined and difficult while—even during the Gorbachev era—generally steady and predictable. But that era has passed. The strains on any new Russian leadership will cause wide shifts in policy and direction. Western leaders will find such shifts disturbing, particularly given the military power that remains in the hands of Russia. The confusion and erratic behavior will be exacerbated by the effort of the commonwealth states to reach agreement on everything from nuclear to monetary policy. In the short- to mid-term, erratic behavior will probably be the pattern, particularly in view of the fact that the new Russian state is competing for capital and investment during a period in which global capital demands far outstrip supply and the Western economies are in recession. Another troubling issue is the potential requirement to use political and military power domestically and on the periphery. Policy debates over use of force are most certain to be resolved differently on each occasion—leading to erratic behavior.

Finally, there remains an age-old question: Is Russia part of Europe? Can and should Russia and its various parts be members of a larger European system? Is it reasonable, as President Mitterrand suggests, to think of a "European Confederation" that extends across Europe to the Urals and beyond? Is it not meaningless to speak, as the Hungarian foreign minister has, of a Europe "from Vladivostok to Vancouver"? The answers of Western Europeans to these questions vary widely, due to ties to Asia and the size, population, and underlying cultural differences. Some argue that Russia—with its proximity, language, music, ballet, its Tolstoy and Chekhov, Peter I and Catherine the Great—is part of European sculture and history. Others retort, if Russia is considered a part of Europe, why not Turkey? What of Central Asia, Siberia, and the Transcaucasus? Is being European mainly a state of mind? How, for that matter, does North America fit into a new, larger Europe?

This debate will increasingly enter into policy discussions as new institutions and concepts are considered to deal with the needs of a new and larger Europe.

The Russians are neurotic—perhaps schizophrenic—about their "Europeanness." They do not want to be rejected and they desperately need Europe's participation in their transformation and development. On the other hand, many Russians still stress their fundamental distinctness—and their spiritual superiority. The new generation of Russians, who have first-hand experience with Western culture, are educated and sophisticated, perhaps a new breed on the historic Russian landscape. This will certainly be an important element as these matters are debated and decided. The traditional split personality has characterized the Russian character for centuries. How both Russians and Western Europeans accommodate this ambivalence will be played out over the coming years, perhaps decades.

EAST-CENTRAL EUROPE

The nations of East-Central Europe* are caught in the traditional vise between the great powers of Europe. They can draw no more solace today from their individual smallness and earnestness than they could in the past.

All of these nations share identical goals: to be free, fully independent, modern European entities and to ultimately become full members of the EC. Yet, almost by definition, each of these nations must pursue its own interests in competition with, or worse, in opposition to its neighbors or its parent state. Although their goals may be the same, the dissonant cacophony of these states threatens to trivialize the idea of nationhood and, more disturbingly, place national survival above respect for human rights and

---

*In discussing this region, the term "nation" is used to describe the existing states from Poland to Bulgaria, as well as the multiple national entities, such as Slovenia and Croatia, within former existing states.

democratic and economic development, and to imperil the principle of peaceful resolution of disputes.

The demons have been released all at once among the nationalities of East-Central Europe. This is happening in a worsening economic environment throughout the region. As a result, the gap between the southern tier (Romania, Bulgaria, former Yugoslavia, and Albania) and the more developed northern tier (Poland, Czechoslovakia, and Hungary) will grow wider over the next decade and beyond. Even though annual rates of growth in some post-communist states are likely to pick up and be even higher than in Western Europe, the standard of living gap will widen between both east and west and north and south. In this competitive situation, nationalism appears to be ever less susceptible to self-restraint and amelioration through education, rising standards of living, the institution of legal systems, and support from international institutions.

The westward policy of every East-Central European nation is motivated not only by the rejection of communism, but by the growing awareness that the West offers the only hope for economic progress and stability. Although the United States is seen as a beacon of democracy, a respected source of political inspiration and economic experience, and the most dependable protective shield, Western Europe is rightly seen as the necessary and desired partner for the future.

The security concerns of East Europeans should not be treated lightly by the West. As small nations, they continue to fear, out of habit but also prescience, the former Soviet empire and Russia, even in its current disarray. Their uncertainty, combined with historic memory, adds to the feeling of insecurity. Many also feel insecure or troubled by adjacent neighbors—whether in the former Yugoslavia, Slovakia, or Transylvania. Finally, a most troubling source of insecurity is the fear that the West, always predominantly drawn to the Russian drama, will devote most available resources to the collapsing Soviet empire and neglect the "smaller" problems of Central Europe. The memory of Munich and Yalta, which twice within living memory determined their fate, continues to cast a foreboding shadow today, whether we like it or not.

The governments of Poland, Czechoslovakia, and Hungary see their salvation through the earliest possible entry into the EC. They want no middle ground or transitional structure to create an anteroom before final entry. They fear that standing in the anteroom will become a permanent limbo. Their new associated member status in the EC offers comforting hope, but is doggedly rejected as the solution.

The southern tier of Eastern Europe—Romania, Bulgaria, Yugoslavia, and Albania—represents a different type of problem. These nations, shaped more by the Ottoman Empire and the "Easternness" of Orthodox Christianity—unlike Poland, Czechoslovakia, Hungary, and Slovenia and Croatia—would be much more difficult to fit into the Europe now taking shape. There are no serious, current discussions about their future admission into a broader EC, which strongly suggests that they will remain on the sidelines or more in the Russian orbit in some new division of Europe. To incorporate them into the broader democratic process will not be easy or speedy, but this issue must be recognized as vitally important. Southeast Europe, after all, is the most explosive part of the continent.

As each of the nations of East-Central Europe seeks to transform itself and shape a future strategy, it finds itself competing with its neighbors. History, language, and geography argue against the emergence of a regional grouping that would bring them together in common purpose and allow them to speak effectively, with more or less a single voice. Experience has shown in other areas, such as the Andean Pact in Latin America, that communications, transportation, and human contact will evolve much more quickly on Europe's East-West axis than North-South among Czechoslovakia, Poland, and Hungary—not to mention Romania, Bulgaria, and the former Yugoslavia. The nations of East-Central Europe will need strong incentives to cooperate with each other as they struggle on.

Subregional efforts such as the Hexagonale initiative of Italy, to develop cooperation among Italy, Hungary, Austria, Poland, Czechoslovakia, and the northern parts of Yugoslavia are helpful integrative ties, building on historic affinities under the Austro-Hungarian Empire. The Hexagonale does have the earmarks of an Italian effort to build up its own special relationships in the region, in the face of expanding German influence. In such a case there is danger that the Hexagonale might rekindle pre–World War II alliances and bilateral friendship agreements that led to the *petites ententes* and countergroups, rather than fostering new structures for international cooperation and development. It is already apparent that the old balance of power politics are at play in the East, recalling the nineteenth-century experiences of these nations. Great restraint and new forms of international accord will be required to head off collisions.

In short, disappointments and despair could dominate the policies of the East-Central European states over the next few years as they face multiple difficult challenges and see the goal of entering the EC receding into the twenty-first century. It is difficult to imagine the EC accepting into its ranks the EFTA nations plus Poland, Czechoslovakia, and Hungary, not to mention Albania, Serbia, Bulgaria, Lithuania, Estonia, and others. A long line of petitioners will be waiting for many years, if not decades. Some steps, however, must be taken soon to fashion a set of institutions for East-Central Europe that will provide a structure for cooperation among themselves and with Western Europe. Some vehicle must be found to help build the legal, physical, and psychological infrastructures to prepare for full entry.

THE UNITED STATES

American interests in Europe have already been reshaped by the events of the past year and will continue to be reshaped by the trends anticipated above. Our power to influence European events has significantly declined. The world today is different from the one for which our European—indeed our entire national security—policy was designed during the Cold War. The United States must reassess its foreign policy priorities and its relationship with Europe. It must make certain that neither the states of Europe nor the American people are confused by its assumptions and actions.

American interests in Europe should be based on the following considerations:

- One nation should not dominate Europe. We must see to it that the Russian state does not again present a major nuclear/military threat to the security of Europe and the United States. We must also reduce the number of nuclear weapons and conventional forces in Germany to a level consistent with the current threat.

- The states of Western Europe should develop political structures and programs that will enable the nations of East-Central Europe to become part of the larger European community and minimize the danger that disorder in the east could lead to broader European instability.

- A strong, democratic EC is vital to the United States. Continuing constructive engagement with the EC, therefore, represents the principal anchor of the United States to internationalism. The United States, despite the end of the Cold War, must not revert to isolationism. Our ties to Europe represent our most familiar and our strongest alliance. They are critical to the evolution of a new, more peaceful international environment.

It is not a contradiction for us to reduce U.S. military commitment of ground forces to Europe. Such action also defines new limits on the U.S. role in European decision-making about European problems.

It will be difficult for the U.S. government to relinquish the guiding role it played so successfully in the Cold War years in holding together and giving policy bite to the NATO alliance. Paranoid pangs at being left out of the decisions of a unified Europe are already arousing anxiety in Washington. This, in turn, is also provoking good-humored and patronizing chiding from European capitals. In short, we have much thinking to do about how best to pursue American interests on the continent.

The first order of business is to prevent a single power dominance of Europe. A related, but not identical issue, is to preclude the resurgence of a militarized Russian power. American leadership in NATO is essential, even at a reduced ground level, to protect the West against such an event. The United States must play the central role in finding creative political and economic incentives to prompt the former Soviet republics to greatly reduce their nuclear arsenals, even through technical assistance in dismantling and destroying them.

Another aspect of ensuring that no single power dominates Europe involves Germany. With the collapse of the Soviet Union, Europe, particularly East-Central Europe, may experience a power vacuum. Ideally, this could lead to a creative process of building up and securing democracy, but it could also result in a crisis caused by the disarray. In such a situation, a large, newly united, economically robust, and politically determined Germany could emerge as the undisputed giant of Europe, pursuing its own agenda among the former satellites.

The demands on Germany in such a situation will not be easily accommodated by the German political leadership. Germany continues to grope for its identity as a world actor, even beyond its economic and trade power. Its passivity in the Gulf war, which confused and angered friends and allies, has been followed by a more assertive German policy in Europe, as manifested in the recognition of Slovenian and Croatian independence to curb Serbian territorial ambitions in former Yugoslav lands. Germany's decision was governed partly by its historical ties to Slovenia and Croatia and partly by Germany's continuing view of the power of nation states.

Western management of an inevitably more dominant Germany calls for the wisest statesmanship. Washington must, in the first place, work closely with Bonn (and soon Berlin). It will also have to work closely—as will the German leadership—with France, Great Britain, and other European states. This will be a long but important process. The French strategy is to use the institutions of Europe to diffuse German power—a strategy that the Germans for now acknowledge and accept. The French strategy is not yet sufficiently persuasive to the British who still remain reluctant to cede sovereignty on many issues, especially in the fiscal and monetary domains. Even though the United States may sympathize with British hesitations about a united Europe, the French view of a Europe united to restrain the German Gulliver is clearly consistent with U.S. interests.

The special partnership that the United States built with Germany during the Cold War is undergoing a change. Yet a key element of U.S. policy must be to build a *new*, close relationship with Germany as part of a strategy to support European unity around the new Germany, to soften German dominance of the disordered Eurasian continent, to share with Germany (not compete with it) in building support structures and economic assistance for the incorporation of East-Central Europe into the new united Europe, and to help manage the rebuilding of Russia.

The Cold War era, indeed most of our recent history, has seen U.S. interests linked to those of Europe through our special relationship with Great Britain. Britain has been our guide and our most sympathetic translator of the European idiom—however accented it may have sounded at times. France has been, in the postwar era, the conceptualizer and ideologist of the new Europe. We have often, with justification, perceived its position as excluding the United States. Appreciation of France's role in defining the new European system does not require the United States to have a special rapport with France. France, however, continues to be the paramount voice of the new Europe, which may grow as North America lowers its profile. It is very much in our interest that

France continues to argue for a united Europe—and that the United States supports this goal.

Germany will become the most important link the United States has to the new Europe. It is important for Germany, for Europe, and for the United States that our postwar partnership deepen. This may not be easy for either side. Because of diminished and less urgent bilateral contacts and the heritage of the U.S. forces in Germany, the younger German generation is often unsympathetic to America. Moreover, the new generation of Americans has not shared in the common energizing bonds of the Marshall Plan, the Berlin Blockade, the Berlin Wall, and the Cold War. As the United States begins to shape a less visible role in Europe, Germany must be our principal partner—and Germany should want no less.

The second set of U.S. interests relates to the incorporation of the states of East-Central Europe into Europe. The question now arises: Does the United States have its own, identifiable interests in Eastern Europe, apart from those of Western Europe, because of our special role in that region after World Wars I and II, because of the large numbers of U.S. citizens who come from that part of the world, and because of our own trade and investment opportunities? The answer is yes, but . . . !

The United States has a political and moral responsibility after the Cold War to ensure that those nations recover their identity, dignity, and well-being. Our major effort, however, must be to pursue our interests in the region by supporting these nations' desire to become a democratic and integral part of Europe. In these respects, our interests coincide with those of Western Europe. This could change, however, if the EC were to exclude East-Central Europe as a de facto policy of the community in order to "deepen" the unity of the twelve plus EFTA. In such a situation, the United States could find itself in the difficult role of becoming the patron of EC expansion toward East-Central Europe, which might imply the weakening of the community.

In view of this potential dilemma the United States and the EC must place at the top of their agenda the development of an intense and generous cooperative venture to promote the security, the economic transformation, and the democratic development of East-Central Europe. Essential to this end is the participation of the United States with Western Europe in programs to improve the transportation and communication links throughout the region, to begin to bring them up to Western standards of living while contributing to the environmental, educational, and cultural needs of the region.

Despite the centrifugal forces at work, the EC may actually achieve a strong unified union in this decade, raising the possibility of a European superpower with its own agenda and presenting a challenge to us all. Such a picture in the early twenty-first century would present the United States with very difficult strategic choices.

A unified Europe could evolve in two different directions. The first might be a powerful EC dominated by Germany, which incorporates from the East only Austria, Poland, Czechoslovakia, Hungary, and perhaps Slovenia, Croatia, and the Baltic states. In this new Europe, the southern tier of Eastern Europe—Romania, Bulgaria, and the other parts of Yugoslavia—would remain outside, as would virtually all of the nations of the former Soviet empire. Such a Europe would define a new form of divisive bloc politics on the European continent, which could present a major economic challenge to the United States and present the Russians a natural opportunity to assert a new Yalta-type division of Europe by extending their zone of influence once again to Eastern Europe.

A second and probably less desirable alternative would be a united, narrowly defined, exclusive Western Europe which tires of the problems of the Eastern states and leaves them all on the outside as the petitioning have-nots of the continent. In this scenario, the security of the eastern region of Europe would be even more severely threatened, and U.S. interests might require the United States to be the advocate of greater European openness toward the East. In such an unlikely scenario, the United States could by the end of this decade find itself supporting a Greater Russian effort to include the poor Slavic nations in the new Europe—thus echoing the era before World War I.

It is unlikely that the EC will achieve full political union in this decade, but its economic strength will continue to grow and trade barriers will diminish as the private sector expands across frontiers. At the same time, many nations will begin to pursue their individual interests, particularly regarding the new nations of the East. For Europe to find coherence, if not unity, new or transformed international institutions will be necessary. The United States will have to assist in shaping these new institutions, but the new institutions may not include the United States as a key player. The challenge to U.S. policymakers will be to help build new European institutions in which the United States does not dominate. For example, organizations such as NATO, CSCE, and the World Bank could eventually spawn new structures to deal specifically with East-Central Europe in which the U.S. role would be subdued, but in which we could exercise our interests through those residual structures where we play a role.

Finally, the relationship between the United States and the nations of Western Europe provides an anchor to U.S. internationalism, since there are no other natural partners with whom we can associate in the continuing quest for a more stable world order. We share more values with Western Europe and more common interests. They are our partners in the UN, the World Bank, the CSCE, and the many other international bodies. The extent to which these bodies function to keep the peace and build cooperation will depend on our capacity to work with the major powers of Europe.

The United States must continue to play a major political role in world affairs while diminishing its military role and becoming a global actor in the financial trade and services arena so vital to our survival as a nation. We will remain partners with the EC and Japan in supporting development and peaceful evolution in the rest of the world. Our collaboration, particularly with Germany, but also with England and France, will continue to be critical to our new path. The existing European mixture of international organizations will be difficult to adapt to the new, more expanded Europe. The U.S. role in this process may be confusing to us and annoying to some Europeans, but it will be important if Europe is to make the institutional leap toward broader coherence.

The new security structures will be the most complex to devise. Much overlap and redundancy will occur in the transition from the post–Cold War era to new forms of managing Europe's inherently disruptive power politics and ethnic nationalism. NATO will continue as insurance against a resurgent Russian power, and as a bonding agent for Germany, but should not be seen or used as a peacekeeping arm for Europe—it should remain a defensive alliance.

The CSCE, to which the United States and Canada belong, has an important role to play. It is the forum in which to air all European issues dealing with verification and transparency for military problems, and for human rights in the new and old democracies. Even though it is not now a security structure, it can serve to impress upon the West the urgency of the problems of the East.

The West European Union (WEU) could become the new European defense pillar providing Western Europe an independent structure for deploying forces on behalf of the EC, although in this case the WEU relationship to NATO forces would have to be clarified. Unless the objectives of the WEU are changed significantly, it cannot provide security to the new democracies of Eastern Europe or be the peacekeeping arm of the EC.

What is lacking for those post-communist nations that have embarked on a course toward democracy but do not belong to NATO is a proper security structure. Neither the CSCE nor the WEU can provide such a structure since the first has no real security role, and the WEU, by definition, is Western European. This missing structure, which cannot be filled by such bodies as the North

Atlantic Cooperation Council, will have to evolve out of other institutions or be created based on the following considerations:

- It should be open only to democratic governments;

- It should be a defensive alliance;

- It should have provisions for peacekeeping;

- It should probably include Western Europe, plus Poland, Czechoslovakia, Hungary, perhaps the Baltic States, Slovenia, and Croatia at the beginning. It should not include Russia in the foreseeable future, or until it is a fully democratic state.

The existing European policymaking bodies must also be expanded to serve the new Europe. The EC is already emerging as the channel for policymaking by the European Twelve leaders on all major issues. The Council of Europe, underutilized and over-discussed, could perhaps become an institutional means to incorporate the new Eastern European democracies into policy discussions. Unless the Council is infused with greater resources and status, however, it can offer only marginal comfort to the outsiders in the East. The Group of Seven annual summits will probably continue to be the most important forum for U.S. involvement in European policy formulation, along with regular bilateral meetings of the chiefs of state.

The final, critical set of existing institutions to be adapted are those dealing with economic, trade, and developmental issues. The OECD is an organization of and for the developed industrialized nations on all continents, but it is difficult to imagine adapting it to assist in the development and transformation of the post-communist societies.

The EC is the ultimate attraction for the nations of the East, but, unless the EC changes its rules and assumptions significantly, full membership is a long way off even for Hungary and Czechoslovakia. The new associated status for Poland, Czechoslovakia, and Hungary has given many Eastern Europeans encouragement, but it will not contribute significantly to regional cooperation in trade and development in the East, nor increase the flow of technical assistance, investments, and aid to the region. The European Bank for Reconstruction and Development (EBRD) will be of some help, but as a regional development bank it can only be a small part of the answer to the needs.

What has been lacking in Europe and the United States is a means of coordinating and expanding support for the transformation and development of the post-communist societies. Some coordination at the initiative of Washington is being undertaken at the technical level in the EC, but this coordination involves neither policy discussions on bilateral programs, nor the various programs carried out by the United States government and private United States foundations or by the variety of international institutions. The Western states and Poland, Czechoslovakia, and Hungary have learned a great deal over the first two years of post-communism about the limits and potential of Western assistance:

- Certain macroeconomic policies to stabilize currencies and the free market process work, others do not;

- Each country in the region, after experimentation, must decide on its own individual course;

- Large scale technical assistance is a vital precondition for transforming the post-communist bureaucracies to enable them to absorb Western assistance more efficiently;

- There are practical obstacles created by donor and recipient states that can and must be overcome—obstacles that in some cases are country-specific and in other cases generic to post-communist societies.

If the West is to expand and maximize its mission of helping the post-communist societies become modern, democratic, free-market states, better coordination and collaboration must be undertaken, either under the auspices of the World Bank or another established institution experienced in development issues. It is possible that a new institution specifically designed to carry out this expanding responsibility may have to be created. We must learn quickly from two years of dealing with Hungary, Poland, and Czechoslovakia as we face the awesome challenges of trying to help to transform the states of the former Soviet Union and those of Southeast Europe.

One wonders how effectively existing European institutions and the United States can deal with the new Russian state and with the other heirs of the former Soviet empire, and with those states of East-Central Europe that do not follow a democratic or a free market path. While the United States and the Western European states should place building democracy, respect for human rights, and free market economic systems in the forefront of their approach to the new Europe, viable bridges must be built to the entire East. We would pay a high price if another great divide in the middle of Europe was someday to become a reality. The new Russian state, however disorderly and autocratic it may become, should not face a West that is stronger, larger, and perceived as threatening at its very borders. This will require great collective wisdom and statesmanship, not an international game of traditional balance of power politics.

Finally, several institutional approaches suggest themselves as elements for a sensible U.S., Western, indeed global course. A strong, continuing U.S. bilateral relationship, even as reactionary times set in in Russia, will be important to help Russia through this decade and beyond. High level contacts, combined with occasional inclusion of the Russian leaders in meetings of the Group of Seven, should help influence the new state's direction. This will involve some political theater but should amount to broad substantive engagement with this complicated new society. Wider collaboration with the new Russian state in the UN, CSCE, and possibly in a future Middle East structure of guarantees will be essential, in addition to the vital ongoing U.S. bilateral efforts with Russia and the other nuclear-armed republics to reduce or eliminate nuclear weapons.

The incorporation of the new Russian state into the World Bank, IMF, and GATT as Russia begins to open up its economy would no doubt provide incentives and guidance to change. Although a coordinated large-scale United States economic assistance program to Russia is not yet appropriate, a ruble stabilization fund in which we would participate would be helpful, and bilateral technical assistance and relief programs will clearly be in order.

While the Russian state, for obvious reasons, will remain the primary focus of U.S. and Western attention, the United States should, nonetheless, build working relations with the other new republics—particularly with Ukraine. Yet we must not be distracted by the variety and disorder on the periphery of the Russian state. The United States simply cannot engage directly the multiple and divisive forces that will be at work over the next decade, though we must have some contact with them. Russia and Ukraine must be objects of the major U.S. programs in the region, and we should be wary of using political pressures on Russia via relations with bordering states. At the same time, while devoting the necessary care to the successor states of the Soviet Union, neglecting the countries of East-Central and Southeast Europe would be a grave mistake. The United States and Western Europe must rise to the challenges of the post-communist era in this complicated region. If we do not, future trouble is certain. If we do, the benefits will be historic.

The United States must, therefore, continue to play a key role in helping the international community manage the disrupting effects of the post-Soviet scene. Reshaping the UN Security Council's role and developing an enlarged UN peacekeeping capability are likely to be major ingredients in the new international community. It will require skill to balance working with the authorities in Moscow on the larger global security issues with expanding contacts and support for new entities in the former empire. Meanwhile, the United States will need to stimulate and encourage the development of the new or changing institutions in Europe while recognizing we may not become the senior member in any of them.

This will be a different role for the United States, which has become accustomed to a position of dominance for half a century in Europe's major decisions. We will continue to provide key support for NATO as long as it is necessary, but on the political front, the Europeans will and should take the lead. The U.S. role is apt to be like that of a sheepdog—working on the fringes, helping to bring decisions to final closure, and sharing in the management and the cost of building democratic societies on the rubble of communism.

APPENDIX: SYMPOSIUM ON THE UNITED STATES AND EASTERN EUROPE, SEPTEMBER 10–11, 1991

Cyrus R. Vance, Chair—*Simpson, Thacher & Bartlett*
Ivo John Lederer, Symposium Director—*A.T. Kearney*
Theresa Weber, Rapporteur—*Council on Foreign Relations*
Audrey McInerney, Rapporteur—*Council on Foreign Relations*

C. Michael Aho—*Council on Foreign Relations*
Ivo Banac—*Yale University*
Seweryn Bialer—*Columbia University*
J.F. Brown—*RAND Corporation*
Janez Drnovsek—*Slovenian member of the Yugoslav Presidency (Ljubljana)*
Charles Gati—*Union College*
Charles Goldman—*ITT Corporation*
Carol Rae Hansen—*Arizona Honors Academy*
Michael Haltzel—*Woodrow Wilson International Center for Scholars*
Robert D. Hormats—*Goldman Sachs International*
William Hyland—Foreign Affairs
Shafiqul Islam—*Council on Foreign Relations*
Laszlo Lang—*Central European Research Center (Budapest)*
Flora Lewis—The New York Times
James Lowenstein—*APCO Associates*
William H. Luers—*The Metropolitan Museum of Art*
Michael Mandelbaum—*Council on Foreign Relations*
Herbert Okun—*Financial Services Volunteer Corps*
Margaret Osmer-McQuade—*Council on Foreign Relations*

Mark Palmer—*Central European Development Corporation*

Ognian Pishev—*Bulgarian Ambassador to the United States*

Nicholas X. Rizopoulos—*Council on Foreign Relations*

Herta Lande Seidman—*Tradenet Corporation*

Elizabeth Sherwood—*Harvard University*

Leonard Silk—The New York Times

Anthony Solomon—*Institute for East-West Security Studies*

Helmut Sonnenfeldt—*The Brookings Institution*

George Soros—*Soros Fund Management*

Balsa Spadijer—*President, Constitutional Court of Serbia (Belgrade)*

Fritz Stern—*Columbia University*

John Temple Swing—*Council on Foreign Relations*

Peter Tarnoff—*Council on Foreign Relations*

Gregory Treverton—*Council on Foreign Relations*

Jan Urban—Lidove Noviny (*Prague*)

Nicholas Wahl—*New York University*

Andrzej Wielowieyski—*Deputy Speaker of the Senate (Warsaw)*

Daniel Yankelovich—*Daniel Yankelovich Group, Inc.*

ABOUT THE AUTHORS

Ivo John Lederer, former professor of East European and Russian history at Yale and Stanford Universities, is Director of the Global Business Policy Council at A.T. Kearney.

J.F. Brown, former director of Radio Free Europe and senior analyst at the RAND Corporation, is Scholar-in-Residence at the RFE/RL Research Institute in Munich.

Robert D. Hormats, former Assistant Secretary of State for Economic and Business Affairs, is Vice Chairman of Goldman Sachs International.

William H. Luers, former U.S. ambassador to Czechoslovakia, is President of the Metropolitan Museum of Art.